COMPASSIONATE FATHER ♥ OR 🔥 CONSUMING FIRE

ENGAGING THE GOD OF THE OLD TESTAMENT

MICHAEL L. BROWN, PHD

COMPASSIONATE FATHER ♥ OR 🔥 CONSUMING FIRE

ENGAGING THE GOD OF THE OLD TESTAMENT

ENGAGING THE GOD OF THE OLD TESTAMENT

CONSUMING FIRE

FATHER ♥ OR

COMPASSIONATE

MICHAEL L. BROWN, PHD

AWKNG
PRESS

Published by AWKNG Press
1000 Riverside Avenue
Jacksonville, FL 32204
awkngpress.com

ISBN: 978-1-955372-02-2 (Hardcover)
978-1-955372-03-9 (ebook)
Library of Congress Control Number: 2021938502

Special Note: Unless otherwise noted, all translations from the Old Testament are my own, made directly from the Hebrew Bible. For the New Testament, I generally used the NIV. It will be seen, however, that all important points can be verified by checking any standard English version. Whenever Hebrew words are cited, I have given the modern Hebrew pronunciation in parentheses, e.g., *rapha'* (pron. rah-FAH), with the accented syllable written in capitals.

CONTENTS

PREFACE
TO SECOND EDITION

The first edition of this book grew out of a lengthy letter I was writing to my sister-in-law, Robin, who was then attending Rhema Bible Training Center in Tulsa, OK. She agreed with her teachers that God is good, that He is a healer of the sick, and that He blesses the righteous. But some of what she heard raised questions for her. Where did the book of Job fit in with all this theology of healing and blessing? And is it true that there is a "permissive tense" (or, "sense") in Hebrew, meaning that God Himself does not bring judgment on anyone but rather "permits" it?

Simply stated, there are hundreds of verses in the Bible, especially in the Old Testament, that at first glance seem to categorically state that at one time or another God put sickness or disease upon His people, or even worse, killed them or caused them to starve to death. What do we do with these verses? Ignore them? Change their meaning? Or do we submit to the plain sense of the text? If so, what does that tell us about the nature of God? In what sense is He "good"?

It is my conviction that many of the standard "faith" answers have robbed the Word of its integrity and have failed to rightly apprehend all of God's message. The emphasis on "intermediate agents" (carrying out God's will, as if this absolves Him) or unknown secret sins (allegedly committed by those who are suffering) has evaded the problem rather than solved it. The question remains: What do we do with the God of the Old Testament who says, "I kill and make alive; I have wounded and it is I Who heal" (Deuteronomy 32:39)?

It is the purpose of this short book to answer this question head on, above all letting God speak for Himself. Back in the 1980s, as I heard lots of Pentecostal-Charismatic Bible teachers talk about God's goodness, I became increasingly disturbed with much of what they were saying, especially when they tried to explain the cause of Job's sufferings, or, more broadly, when they spoke about the God of the Old Testament. In more recent years, as attacks on the Bible have become more common, the

God of the Old Testament has been portrayed as a moral monster, causing many Christians, especially young people, to question their faith. How do we answer their heartfelt questions?

It is my firm belief that true faith will always accept all of God's truth, regardless of denominational barriers or human restraints. True faith will never compromise Scripture, but instead will be totally founded on God's revelation alone.

I have written this study so as to produce right, uncompromising faith in the integrity of the Word and in the faithfulness and consistency of the Lord. And interestingly, it was friends who emphasized God's goodness who urged me to put this in writing back in 1985. In the current edition, I have revised some sections and sharpened the arguments, but the basic text and message remain the same. And I appreciate AWKNG Press for taking an interest in making this updated volume available to a new set of readers.

For those wanting a full-length, academic study of divine healing, especially in the Old Testament, I recommend my study, *Israel's Divine Healer* (Grand Rapids: Zondervan, 1995). For my response to those who deny the gifts of the Spirit for today, see *Authentic Fire: A Response to*

John MacArthur's Strange Fire (Lake Mary, FL: Excel Publishers, 2013). For my full views on Job, see *Job: The Faith to Challenge God; A New Translation and Commentary* (Peabody, MA: Hendrickson, 2019).

With a spirit of humility and reverence for God, then, I offer this study to all interested readers. Understand that it is not my desire to attack brothers and sisters who differ with me or to insult their sincerely held beliefs. As co-laborers with the Lord, we must seek to build up and not tear down; we must fill up the supply where our co-workers may lack. It is with the purpose of "filling up" an existing gap that these pages now follow. I challenge you to hear the Word with your heart and mind wholly open to God. May the Holy Spirit guide us into all truth!

Michael L. Brown,
FEBRUARY 2021

THE FEARS OF THE
WICKED ARE REALIZED,

BUT THE FEARS OF THE
RIGHTEOUS DISAPPEAR
INTO NOTHING,

FOR GOD IS WITH THE
RIGHTEOUS.

CHAPTER 1

THE PROBLEM

Anyone who has had a clear revelation of Jesus the Healer and Restorer of His people has come to know firsthand that God is a good God and that He loves to bless His children. The Father is no longer seen as a tyrant out to get us, seeking to condemn us to hell and destroy us. We now know that it is His revealed will and pleasure to make us whole in mind, body, and spirit, and sickness and disease are clearly understood as works of the devil (e.g., Luke 13:16; Acts 10:38). It is Satan who makes us sick and Jesus Who makes us well. No longer will we praise God for what the destroyer has done. This is certainly the teaching of the New Testament.

When we turn back to the revelation of God to the children of Israel in the Old Testament, we again see the Lord as the One Who forgives *all* our sins and heals *all* our diseases (Ps. 103:3). He takes sickness out of our midst (Exodus 23:25-26; Deuteronomy. 7:15), and so we often quote the wonderful promise, "I am the Lord your Healer" (Exodus 15:26; the Hebrew for "Healer" is *rophe'ka* [pronounced roh-FEH-kha]; "Jehovah Rapha," which is commonly quoted, means "the Lord healed"). Many people have been restored to health by speaking this very Scripture in faith.

Put or Permit?

Yet for all this, some immediate questions arise. When we read Exodus 15:26 in its entirety, we see that God says He will not put any of the sicknesses upon us which *He put* upon the Egyptians. And although many faith teachers have stated that the Hebrew word for "put" means "allow," this simply is not true. The Hebrew root *sim* (pron. SEEM), used 586 times in the Hebrew Bible, always means "put, place, set, or make," and *never once* means "allow." In fact, it is incorrect to say that this or any other Hebrew verb is ever used in a "permissive tense," for no such "tense" exists in Hebrew! (In fact, "tense" has to do with time; what these teachers mean is a "permissive sense," but that is not accurate either – and I say this as someone with a bachelor's degree in Hebrew and a master's and Ph.D. in Semitic languages; I also own every single major, scholarly grammar of the Hebrew language, and I assure you that the "permissive sense" does not exist.) Thus, according to this Scripture, *it was the Lord Who put sicknesses upon the Egyptians*. Note also that in Exodus 5:14-11:10, God takes responsibility for all of the ten plagues which were sent upon Egypt (see the discussion in Chapter 3).

Turning back to Genesis 20:17, the first reference to healing in the Bible, we see from verse 18 that Abraham prayed for the healing of Abimelech's household "because the Lord had completely shut up all the wombs of the household of Abimelech." In other words, since God closed the wombs (notice no intermediate agent is mentioned), He alone could open them and restore fertility to these people.

Another wonderful verse often quoted is Isaiah 54:17, "No weapon formed against you shall prosper," but according to the second half of verse 16, God says "it is I Who have created the destroyer to wreak havoc." In fact, this verse sounds very much like Isaiah 45:7: "I form the light and create darkness; I bring prosperity and create disaster; I, the Lord, do all these things" (NIV). How can this be?

GOD OF LIFE
OR GOD OF DEATH?

But this is only the beginning. In Deuteronomy 32:39, God categorically states, "See now that I, I am He, and there is no god with Me. I kill and I make alive; I have wounded, and it is I Who heal — there is none to deliver from My hand." Amos 3:6b asks the rhetorical question, "Will there be disaster in the city if the Lord has not done it?", while Lamentations 3:38 asks, "Don't both calamities and good proceed from the mouth of the Most High?" And understand that the inspired writers expected a definite answer of "yes" to both of their questions.

If we remember the numerous cases in the New Testament where demonic possession was the cause of deafness, dumbness, or blindness, then how do we understand the Lord's words to Moses in Exodus 4:11: "Who made man's mouth? Or Who makes deaf people, or dumb, or seeing, or blind? Isn't it I, the Lord?" (i.e., "I, the Lord, have done it")?

How do we deal with the things that God says about Himself in the book of Hosea? "I am like a moth to Ephraim, like rot to the people of Judah" (Hosea 5:12); "I will be like a lion to Ephraim, like a great lion to Judah. I will tear them to pieces and go away; I will carry them off with no one to rescue them" (5:14). "Even if they rear children, I will bereave them of every one" (9:12a). "Even if they bear children, I will slay their cherished offspring" (9:16b). "I will be like a lion to them, like a leopard I will lurk by the path. Like a bear robbed of her cubs, I will attack them and rip them open; like a lion I will devour them—a wild animal will tear them apart. You are destroyed, Israel, because you are against Me, your Helper" (13:7-9, NIV). Is it possible to reconcile these verses with the famous words of the apostle John, "God is love"?

Yet the problem becomes compounded when we read in Deuteronomy 28 about the blessings for obedience (vv. 1-14) and the curses for disobedience (vv. 15-68). Even though, "Christ has redeemed us from the curse of the law, having been made a curse for us" (Galatians 3:13), and, therefore, we can praise God for the blessings He sends, how do we explain the fact that it was the Lord Who sent the curses in the Old Testament?

Listen carefully to these almost unbelievable statements recorded in Deuteronomy 28. "The Lord will let loose against you calamity, panic, and frustration in all you undertake. The Lord will make pestilence cling to you. The Lord will strike you with consumption, fever, and inflammation, with scorching heat and drought, with blight and mildew; they shall hound you until you perish"

(vv. 20-22). "The Lord will make the rain of your land dust. The Lord will put you to rout before your enemies" (vv. 24-25). "The Lord will strike you with the Egyptian inflammation, with hemorrhoids, boil-scars, and itch, from which you shall never recover. The Lord will strike you with madness, blindness, and dismay" (vv. 27-28). "The Lord will afflict you at the knees and thighs with a severe inflammation, from which you shall never recover from the sole of your foot to the crown of your head" (v. 35). "The Lord will inflict extraordinary plagues upon you and your offspring, strange and lasting plagues, malignant and chronic diseases. He will bring back upon you all the sicknesses of Egypt which you dreaded so, and they shall cling to you. Moreover, the Lord will bring upon you all the other diseases and plagues that are not mentioned in this book of Teaching, until you are wiped out" (vv. 59-61). "And as the Lord once delighted in making you prosperous and many, so will the Lord now delight in causing you to perish and in wiping you out" (v. 63, New Jewish Publication Society Version).

There is no more devastating account of destruction anywhere in the Bible (or, for that matter, probably in all literature). The total effect of these verses is overwhelming. And yet it was the Lord Who over and over again claimed to be causing these disasters to take place. Surely none of us would even flinch if it was the devil whose name occurred over and over again. But the

Lord? Our merciful heavenly Father, Who is all light, with no darkness in Him at all (1 John 1:5)?

There must be an answer that will sufficiently explain how the God Whom we love and worship could be described in such horrifying ways. There must be a way to explain why the Lord, our Redeemer, our Healer, and our Restorer, would so graphically take credit for all kinds of calamities and pains. And of course, there is an answer, one which will be detailed and discussed in the following chapters. But first we must examine some current teaching regarding the book of Job.

What About Job?

Sadly enough, the exegetical gymnastics performed in order to deal with the apparent theological contradictions in Job have not really been a credit to the godly leaders who have wrestled with these problems. Of course, it is praiseworthy to endeavor to protect and defend the honor and glory of God by reexamining certain difficult portions of the Word, but it is far better to speak the truth as we have it and allow God to defend Himself. The fact of the matter is that when we unintentionally impose our own convictions on the Word so as to avoid any possible scriptural misunderstandings, we actually bring reproach to the Lord by not being faithful witnesses. Since most of what we will now look at is very familiar teaching in some circles, I would encourage you to ask the Holy Spirit for a fresh understanding, because the Spirit will always bear witness with the Word rightly interpreted.

It is commonly assumed that Satan (Hebrew *haSatan*, pron. hah-sah-TAHN, "the adversary" or "the accuser") instigated all of Job's sufferings. This is only partially true, since even though Satan was the instigator (Job 1:9-11, 2:4-5), it was the Lord Who brought Job to the devil's attention (Job 1:8, 2:3). Thus, the first move was made by God.

More important is the contention that Job was "operating in fear" (Job 3:25 is normally quoted here) and that he was "offering sacrifices in fear" (Job 1:5), thus allowing the enemy to have access to him. A careful study will show that this position is not correct. (The truth be told, it is downright insulting to Job and undermines the very message of the book.)

According to Job 1:1, Job was "blameless and upright, fearing God and departing from evil." This is the ideal description of a godly man in the Hebrew language. In fact, in Old Testament thought, anyone who walked in "the fear of the Lord" had no fear of anything at all (see Proverbs 14:26-27, "In the fear of the Lord is a strong fortress, and for one's children it will be a refuge. The fear of the Lord is a fountain of life, to escape from the snares of death"). And according to verse 1, Job did walk in the fear of the Lord. Also, Ezekiel 14:14 and 14:20 refer to Job as an extremely righteous man, and James 5:11 speaks of Job as being blessed because he persevered in the face of suffering. These are not descriptions of a man bound by fear!

The author of Job was eager to illustrate Job's godliness in action, and he therefore mentioned Job's habit of regularly sacrificing for his children just in case they had sinned against God. In a true spirit of intercession, and as patriarchal priest of his home, Job prayed and offered sacrifices so as to protect his children from any foolish moments of defiance against the Lord. How many Christian parents, having become negligent in their intercessory prayers for their children, have suddenly and unexpectedly found out that their precious offspring have died of a drug overdose or a drunken car wreck or a suicide? Contrary to those who allege that Job offered sacrifices in fear and not in faith, the Word plainly shows that he was doing everything he could to keep disaster far from himself or his own (see also Job 31:23). The fact that Job did not make our contemporary "faith confessions" does not mean that he was walking in fear.

Job 3:25 states poetically that the greatest disasters feared by Job had come upon him. It does *not* teach that Job walked in this fear, nor does it state that this supposed fear caused him to have a hole in his defenses. In fact, if we carefully study Job 3:25, we will see once again that "the truth will set us free."

THE FEARS OF THE RIGHTEOUS

The first half of Job 3:25 states that the "fear" which Job "feared" had come upon him, and both the noun "fear" and the verb "feared" come from the same Hebrew root, *pakhad* (pronounced pah-KHAHD). Furthermore, the noun literally means both "fear" and "the thing feared," in other words, "disaster." The second half of the verse says that the thing Job "dreaded" visited him.

According to Proverbs 1:26, God will mock those who despise His law when their *pakhad* (i.e., "their fear-disaster") comes upon them (see also v. 27 and 10:24, "What the wicked dread will come upon him"). But the obedient will dwell securely, safe from terrible *pakhad* (again "fear-disaster"; see Proverbs 1:33). In Deuteronomy 28:60, God promised to bring on apostate Israel all the diseases of Egypt which they "dreaded" (same word as in Job 3:25b), but for the faithful He promised to remove these very sicknesses from their midst (Exodus 15:26; Deuteronomy 7:15).

Do you see the point? The fears of the wicked are realized, but the fears of the righteous disappear into nothing, for God is with the righteous. Thus, according to Psalm 91:5, we need not fear the nighttime fear (again *pakhad*), for what we fear will not come upon us if we trust in and abide under the covering mercy of God. Moses said in Deuteronomy 9:19, "For I was in dread because of the burning wrath of the Lord when He was angry enough to destroy you – yet the Lord heard my voice this time too." Hallelujah! Moses was scared stiff because he thought that God would totally wipe out Israel. But did He? No, absolutely not! He was merciful and gracious, and so, by the grace of God, *Moses's fears were not realized.*

One of the greatest preachers of our age stated that when God told him to greatly expand his ministry, he was afraid and worried that he would fail. But did he? No, not at all; in fact, his ministry abundantly prospered. Another great man of God said that he feared going ahead with some key meetings because he was convinced that no one would show up. Yet his fears vanished into the air, for God was with him. One dear brother even stated that he feared his own child would die of a dreaded disease, but his fears fell away, and his son lived healthy and strong.

You see, these men had their *pakhad*s, but the disasters which they feared did not come upon them. When Paul feared for the Galatians (Galatians 4:11, "I fear for you, that somehow I have wasted my efforts on you"), were his fears realized? No! When he feared for the Thessalonians (1 Thessalonians 3:5b, "I was afraid that in some way the tempter might have tempted you and our efforts may have been useless"), were his fears realized? No! Why? Because he loved God and kept His commandments (see also 2 Corinthians 7:5-7).

What a shock to poor Job, when, in spite of his obedience, his fears came upon him. This was the exact opposite of what he expected (see Job 31:1-23; because he feared God's punitive judgments for sin and disobedience, he was careful to live a life of detailed obedience to the Almighty). Yet, in spite of this disaster, he hung in there.

When you really stop and think about it, trusting God frees you from fear, but believing that "whatever you fear will come upon you" actually paralyzes your faith. In fact, you'll probably end up fearing your fears instead of fearing God. So then, don't fear your fears, for, ultimately, *fear is based on lies*. Don't give your fears any substance by dwelling on them, for they will *never materialize* if you walk in obedience to God and trust His holy Word. His promises are sure! You'll get rid of fear when you get into faith.

All this helps to explain the fact that if the Lord did not permit Satan to afflict Job, then the devil would not have been able to penetrate the divine hedge which surrounded him (Job 1:10-12). Furthermore, the Lord Himself told Satan, "you incited Me against him to destroy him without a cause" (Job 2:3). Yes, *without a cause*! Why then do we find it necessary to invent causes when the Lord says that there were none? (For a detailed discussion of this passage, along with the entire book of Job, I refer you again to my 2019 commentary on Job titled *Job: The Faith to Challenge God: A New Translation and Commentary*.)

Invented Causes

Some people have argued, "Job must have been guilty, because according to the Word, 'the curse causeless shall not come'" (Proverbs 26:2, KJV). But that is not what Proverbs really says. The whole verse reads: "Like a fluttering sparrow or a darting swallow, an undeserved curse does not *come to rest*" (NIV, my italics). Do you see it? The curse could not stay on Job. God *had* to lift it off, because "an undeserved curse does not come to rest." Also, it is possible to translate this phrase as, "an undeserved curse shall *come back* to him," i.e., to the one who sent it. In other words, it will backfire. And that's just what happened in the book of Job. Satan tried to curse Job, a righteous man, and it backfired on him. Job blessed God and ended up the winner; Satan cursed Job and ended up the loser.

All this is clear. Nonetheless, people still try and find new causes for Job's sufferings. Some have said that he suffered because he married the wrong woman. This is inferred from his wife's intemperate speech in Job 2:9 where she bids Job to curse God and die. Yet, in all fairness, the poor woman had just lost all of her children, all of her possessions, all of her savings, and all of her husband's health and reputation, and in a moment of time at that. Is it so inconceivable that she got mad for a minute and blew her top? (It's also possible that she was concerned for Job's dignity, urging him to curse God, which would then bring about his death and the end of the ordeal.) Job himself got pretty angry as the debate with his friends wore on. But more to the point is the fact that Job's wife (there is *no* biblical evidence to say that she died and that God gave Job a new wife) gave him ten more blessed children, and they apparently lived "happily ever after" (Job 42:12-15). If she was part of the Lord's blessing, Job's latter end more than his beginning, then she must have been a godly woman.

Did Job Blaspheme?

Unfortunately, there is one more invented cause for Job's suffering, and although I would rather not even mention it, it is too well known to be ignored. I refer to the notion that Job blasphemed when he spoke his famous words, "The Lord gave and the Lord took away," since, the argument runs, "We know that God never takes away from his children." (I have heard that quote too many times to think that it was just one man's oversimplification of the facts.) According to this viewpoint, even though these words were spoken after Job's sufferings had begun, it reflected the wrong attitude in which he had been walking. So runs the argument.

Yet I must honestly say that there is not one thread of evidence to support this opinion. Verse 22 of Job chapter 1, which is God's inspired commentary on verse 21, says, "In all this Job did not sin with his lips or charge God with anything unseemly." In fact, the Hebrew word *tiphlah* (pronounced tif-LAH), translated "unseemly," literally means "something unsavory," here with reference to God's character. In other words, when Job said "the Lord takes away," he was not saying anything offensive or wrong about God (we will explain this in Chapter 3). Also, the Lord gave testimony on His servant's behalf in Job 2:3, stating that Job was still blameless and upright, fearing God, turning from evil, and maintaining his integrity. God even repeated that there was no one like Job in all the earth. Do we dare disagree with God's viewpoint? Why didn't *He* say that Job was "in ignorance"?

In Job 2:10, after Job had expressed willingness to receive either good *or* bad from the Lord's hand, it is emphasized again that he did not sin in what he said.

Also, in Job 42:11, the inspired author relates that after Job's captivity was turned, his former friends and relatives came to comfort and console him (*not* "bemoan him," as in the KJV) over all the calamity *which the Lord had brought upon him*. Note again that this was the Holy Spirit's comment, not someone else's opinion. Finally, it must be stated that God was not displeased with Job at all until he departed from his great statements of faith in Job 1:21 and 2:10 (we will discuss all these points in greater detail in Chapter 4).

It should be clear then that if we are to maintain our views of God as *the good God*, we must seek answers to the questions raised in this chapter on new and different grounds. Since it is the object of this study to create in us a right and proper faith by lifting up the Word in its integrity, and not to magnify doubt, we must proceed immediately to the heart of our discussion.

GOOD HEALTH & LONG LIFE ARE ALWAYS PROMISED AS COVENANT BLESSINGS,

WHILE DISEASE & PREMATURE DEATH ARE ALWAYS ENUMERATED AS COVENANT CURSES.

CHAPTER 2

THE BLESSINGS OF OBEDIENCE AND THE JUSTICE OF GOD

The perceptive reader of the previous chapter will no doubt have begun to realize that all of the divine judgments referred to came about as a result of sin and disobedience. All the curses of Deuteronomy 28 were repeatedly explained as being the direct and inevitable consequences of refusing to hearken to the voice of God (see Deuteronomy 28:15, 45, and 58; see also Deuteronomy 27:14-26). In the book of Hosea, where the Lord depicted Himself as a wild animal about to tear Israel to pieces (this, by the way, is what actually happened in 722 BC when the Assyrians destroyed the Northern Kingdom of Israel and exiled many of its inhabitants), the people were reminded that it was their sins which had laid them low (Hosea 14:1). The plagues which came upon the Egyptians were directly related to the hard-hearted and oppressive policies of the Pharaoh (Genesis 15:13-14).

All of these statements lead to a very important point: *nowhere in the entire Bible has God ever promised to bring sickness and calamity upon His obedient children.* With striking regularity, *good health* and *long life* are always promised as covenant *blessings*, while *disease* and *premature death* are always enumerated as covenant *curses*. The notion that we should praise God for wasting sickness and sudden disaster (in other words, for the covenant *curses*) is absolutely foreign to Old Testament thought, since the covenant curses were clearly understood as being the fruit of *sin*. It is one thing to praise the Lord for Who He is in the midst of calamity. It is another thing entirely to praise Him for the specific disaster. (For Job 1:21, see Chapter 4.) When Miriam sinned against the Lord and against Moses in Numbers 12, the man of God did not praise God for his sister's leprosy, but he prayed for her healing. When the Psalmist perceived that he was suffering affliction because of his sin, he did not thank God for the condition; instead, he cried out, "Lord, have mercy on me; heal me, for I have sinned against You!" (Psalm 41:4; see also Psalm 6:1-2, Psalm 38, and Psalm 51:8). Psalm 103:3 strategically joins together the *forgiveness of sins* and the *healing of diseases*. This immediately sheds light on two important New Testament passages, namely Matthew 9:1-8 (especially v. 6) and James 5:14-16 (especially the end of v. 15 and the beginning of v. 16).

Sickness and Sin

In the Old Testament, it was broadly acknowledged that *sin in general* was the ultimate cause of all human suffering, even though it was understood that not all sickness was the direct result of *specific sins*. Therefore, when Jesus dealt with the sin problem once and for all by nailing it to the cross, He provided the final and ultimate remedy for all human suffering: the blood of Jesus the Messiah. The Gospels consistently portray the ministry of Jesus in terms of restoring back to mankind what sin and Satan had robbed. Thus, whenever the gospel is truly declared in faith and power, miracles of restoration *must* take place.

But this topic takes us too far afield right now. Let us only reiterate that in Old Testament thought two very clear lines were drawn: blessings for obedience and curses for disobedience (for the specific questions raised in the Book of Job, see Chapter 4).

I once spent more than five hours with a well-educated young Baptist pastor, discussing sickness and healing. He freely acknowledged that all of the horrible things which he was trained to praise God for are viewed by the Bible as the consequences of the fall of man and the resultant judgments of God. Therefore, those who would refer to the verses gathered together in Chapter 1 in order to prove that the Lord would put sickness and disease upon us have entirely missed the point. *Not once in the Scriptures is it recorded that the Lord put sickness and disease upon His obedient children.* Nowhere is it said that the Lord afflicted His faithful children with such conditions. These afflictions were seen as part of the curse from which, thank God, we have been redeemed.

Of course, I am not saying that if we are sick, we are therefore in disobedience. Rather, I am only pointing out that many opponents of divine healing have misused and misinterpreted many of the verses we cited, and it is against these misinterpretations that teachers of divine healing have reacted. Consequently, they wanted to emphasize that the Lord would never, in the past, present, or future, afflict His children with sickness.

Yet these faith teachers have also missed the point. You see, even if we do acknowledge that, according to the Old Testament, God sent curses upon His apostate people (rather than on His obedient people), this fact does not alter our preaching at all, since Jesus paid for our sin and apostasy, and it is the Father's revealed will and desire to bless us with good things. The cross now declares that total healing of mind, body, and spirit (the Hebrew concept of healing recognized no significant divisions here) is the purchased possession of the people of God. To say that the Lord sent judgments upon His disobedient children in the Old Testament is not to say that He is now out to get us!

God's Holy Character

This leads us to our second point, namely the justice (and holiness) of God with regard to the blessings and the curses. It is important to remember that our God is wholly righteous, and that there is no taint of unrighteousness, iniquity, or immorality in Him. Whatever He does is pure and without fault, for "all His ways are just" (Deuteronomy 32:4). Even when we speak of the love of God, we are speaking of a powerful moral force, for God's love rejoices only in truth (1 Corinthians 13:6). It is directly and uncompromisingly opposed to all evil, and it is most clearly revealed to us in the cross – the death of the Lord Jesus to satisfy the Father's justice (Romans 3:25-26), the free offer of salvation to satisfy His mercy (Romans 5:8). That is truly the love of God, justice, and mercy rolled into one, poured out to redeem a disobedient people.

The connection between the righteous love of God and the problem that we are discussing is simply this: by making the Lord out to be some nice old "grandfather" figure who wouldn't even think of hurting a fly, we have unconsciously compromised His holy character. As one writer aptly put it, He is not just our "celestial buddy." He is the Sovereign Lord (Hebrew *'adonay*, pronounced ah-doh-NAI), the all-powerful Ruler, the King of kings, and the Lord of lords! His name is Yahweh, "He Who brings all things into being," and He is a consuming fire (Deuteronomy 4:24, Hebrews 12:29)!

The apostle Paul is very clear on this matter: "Behold therefore the goodness and severity of God: on them which fell, severity; but toward thee, goodness, if thou continue in his goodness: otherwise thou also shalt be cut off" (Romans 11:22, KJV). John the Immerser spoke of Jesus in very similar terms when he described the Lord's purifying and separating ministry: "His winnowing fork is in his hand, and he will clear his threshing floor, gathering the wheat into his barn and burning up the chaff with unquenchable fire" (Matthew 3:12). In fact, the scene at the end of the age will be very similar: "God is just: He will pay back trouble to those who trouble you, give relief to you who are troubled, and to us as well. This will happen when the Lord Jesus is revealed from heaven in blazing fire with his powerful angels" (2 Thessalonians 1:6-7).

Come Lord Jesus!

Maybe for the first time it is becoming clear to you that when we pray, "Even so, come, Lord Jesus!" (Revelation 22:20), we are actually praying for the day in which the ungodly will be "punished with everlasting destruction from the presence of the Lord, and from the glory of his power" (2 Thessalonians 1:9).

You see, *God's judgment is a saving act*. The judgment of the wicked means the salvation of the righteous, and the judgment of the world means the salvation of the Church. That is why the psalmist wrote: "Sing to the Lord a new song. Shout before King Yahweh. For He comes to judge the earth, and He will judge the world in righteousness, and the peoples in justice" (Psalm 98:1, 6, and 9).

Of course, I fully understand that only a heartless man would rejoice at the thought of millions of people going to hell. Sometimes the knowledge that even *one* soul is perishing becomes too much to bear, especially if that one soul is someone we know. Yet in the final analysis we must agree that "God is just," and when all of His self-sacrificing efforts to snatch a soul from damnation have been rejected, we must say, "Amen, Lord, Your will be done."

When the curses were pronounced on Mount Ebal in Deuteronomy 27, the people were to respond together and say, "Amen" (which means, "So be it"). In this way, they were acknowledging that if someone violated the covenant, then he or she would get what they deserved. In the book of Revelation, after God's judgments are poured out, the heavenly chorus bears witness saying, "Just and true are your ways" (Revelation 15:3); "You are just in these judgments" (16:5); "True and just are your judgments" (16:7); "Rejoice over her (Babylon), O heaven! Rejoice, saints and apostles and prophets! God has judged her for the way she treated you" (18:20); "For true and just are his judgments" (19:2). In our zeal to proclaim the mercy of God, let us not forget His justice. When Abraham interceded for Sodom, he had no problem with God slaying the *wicked* (i.e., with God's justice); his prayer was that the Lord would not slay the *righteous with* the wicked. He knew that the Judge of all the earth would do right (Genesis 18:25).

And this leads to a statement that might be startling to some. The fact that the Lord judges the guilty makes Him a *good God*. The fact that Satan destroys the innocent makes him a *bad devil*. One is an expression of life and light. The other is an expression of death and darkness. And never the twain shall meet.

FIGHTING AGAINST GOD

You see, God is not fickle, as we so often are. He is

always totally *for* righteousness and totally *against* unrighteousness, totally *for* truth and totally *against* lies, totally *for* mercy and totally *against* cruelty. He is not on our side one day and against us another day, for He does not change. However, we do change. He is always going in one direction, and if we follow Him in faith, then He is for us; if we oppose Him in unbelief, then He is against us, but not because He changed His course. It is we who changed our course. The Lord was merely continuing down the path that He laid out for Himself in eternity past. It is the path of light, life, and love, the course of eternal blessing for all of His people. Those who travel the road to hell find themselves going against God Himself.

What then is the result of a head-to-head confrontation with the living God? Listen to the words of the Lord Jesus in Revelation 2:21-23 regarding the false prophetess Jezebel: "I have given her time to repent of her immorality, but she is unwilling. So I will cast her on a bed of suffering, and I will make those who commit adultery with her suffer intensely, unless they repent of her ways. I will strike her children dead. Then all the churches will know that I am he who searches hearts and minds, and I will repay each of you according to your deeds." (The crucial phrase "unless they repent" is explained by the Lord in Revelation 3:19: "Those whom I love I rebuke and discipline. So be earnest and repent.") In other words, love which does not say, "Stop! Turn back! You're going the wrong way!" is not really love at all. Paul turned an unrepentant brother over to Satan for the destruction of his flesh, so that in the end his spirit might be saved (1 Corinthians 5:5).

If you ask the question, "Does God use intermediate agents in the accomplishing of His judgments?", the answer is, "Yes, of course He does." But this does not diminish the fact that He Himself takes full and complete responsibility for these acts, and by them He teaches us the consequences of crossing Him. "It is a fearful thing to fall into the hands of the living God" (Hebrews 10:31).

In the next chapter, we will discuss this point in detail, that is, why God was so emphatic in His declarations that He alone wounded and healed and that He alone killed and made alive. But first let us state again the two main points of this chapter. First, nowhere in the Old Testament did God ever threaten to bring sickness or disaster upon His obedient children. His revealed will was always blessing, not cursing, for those who followed Him. Therefore, those who would point to certain Old Testament judgments to prove that the Lord might so afflict His faithful church have not "rightly handled the Word" (2 Timothy 2:15). Second, although we should not praise God for the covenant curses in and of themselves, we must always remember that He is a just God, and His judgments are always righteous and praiseworthy. The Lord is against those who willfully refuse His grace, and He will put up all necessary roadblocks in order to turn them from their sins. If they die in rebellion against God we must ultimately say, "So be it, Lord, for Your ways are just and true." While we do not delight in a sinner's suffering, we acknowledge that the Lord is right in repaying each (unsaved) man according to his deeds.

"TURN BACK TO ME!
FOR ✝ALTHOUGH
I HAVE WOUNDED, ✖

IT IS MY DESIRE
TO HEAL; 🤍

THOUGH IT IS
I WHO KILLED, 🔥

IT IS MY WILL
TO MAKE YOU ALIVE."

CHAPTER 3

GOD
AND THE GODS

"Hear O Israel, the Lord is our God, the Lord alone" (Deut. 6:4). This verse stands as the central revelation of God to His Old Testament people. It precedes the admonition to love Him with all the heart, soul, and strength, for without this knowledge of the Lord, Israel could not have been a special and separate people. There was nothing more crucial to the chosen nation than the realization that Yahweh alone was God.

The Hebrew word translated "alone" is *'ekhad* (pron. eh-KHAD), and it is usually rendered by our English word "one." Yet there are times when it clearly means "only one," or "that one alone," as is the case in 1 Chronicles 29:1 where David said, "Solomon my son, *whom alone* God hath chosen, is yet young and tender . . ." (KJV). This is also the meaning in Deuteronomy 6:4: "The Lord is our God, the Lord *alone*." In reality, Moses was not trying to teach the people that Yahweh was one. All the gods that the heathen worshiped were each believed to be one. Moses was saying that Yahweh alone was God, that there was no other god but Him, and that were not different Yahwehs in different regions. The apostle Paul expressed the same thought in 1 Corinthians 8:4: "So then, about eating food sacrificed to idols: We know that an idol is nothing at all in the world *and that there is no God but one*" (see also 1 Corinthians 8:5-6). This has always been the confession of God's people.

The primary battle fought by the Old Testament prophets, priests, and kings was to get the children of Israel to know that there was only one God, Yahweh, and that the gods of the nations were no gods at all. When Moses was on Mount Sinai for forty days and nights, he returned to the camp only to find that the people had made an idol to worship (Exodus 32), and this, just weeks after they had seen the Lord's miracles in Egypt and had passed through the Red Sea.

In the book of First Kings, we read the striking account of the confrontation of Elijah and the false prophets of Baal (in Hebrew, Baal means "master"). Chapter 18, verse 21, tells us that when Elijah challenged the crowd to make a decision between the Lord and Baal, "the people answered him not a word." Can you imagine a church so apostate that when asked to choose between Jesus and the devil that they don't say anything at all? Yet this was the condition of Israel in the days of Ahab and Jezebel. It was only when the Lord answered by fire from heaven that "all the people saw, and they fell on their faces and said 'The Lord, He is God. The Lord, He is God'" (1 Kings 18:39).

Two centuries later, when a spirit of repentance fell upon the godly king Josiah, this young man had to purify the temple of the Lord from an amazing assortment of idolatrous abominations. Second Kings 23:4-7 tells us that, "The king ordered Hilkiah the high priest, the priests next in rank and the doorkeepers to remove from the temple of the Lord all the articles made for Baal and Asherah and all the starry hosts. . . . He did away with the idolatrous priests appointed by the kings of Judah to burn incense on the high places of the towns of Judah . . . . He also tore down the quarters of the male shrine prostitutes that were in the temple of the Lord, the quarters where women did weaving for Asherah" (NIV; for more details, read vv. 5-28 and 2 Chronicles 34).

It is almost unbelievable to consider that less than one

hundred years earlier King Hezekiah had performed a similar purge on this very temple (2 Chronicles 29), and that at least Isaiah, Micah, Hosea, and Amos had already completed their prophetic ministries. It is plain to see that the nations of Israel and Judah led a treacherous, see-saw existence which often ended up in total apostasy for all but the small godly remnant. Isaiah himself named one of his sons Shear-Jashub (pron. sh'-AR-ya-SHOOV), "only a remnant will return" (or "repent").

In light of these facts, we begin to understand why God often commanded the Israelites to totally wipe out the godless nations whose land they were possessing. They were to put them under the ban (Hebrew *kherem*, pron. KHEH-rem) and devote them to the Lord by destruction. If it seemed cruel and harsh, they were to be reminded that the land itself was vomiting out these sinful nations, and if the people of Israel allowed them to remain in the land, then the Israelites would also become corrupted and fall under the same curse (Leviticus 18:24-28). If the succeeding generations barely survived as the people of God, in spite of the fact that Joshua drove out and killed most of the pagan nations, then it is clear that Israel would have become totally assimilated to the world if they allowed these peoples to co-inhabit the land with them (see also Judges 2:1-3).

God's Separate People

It is crucial to understand why it was so important for God to keep for Himself a separate people. According to Galatians 4:4, "When the time had fully come, God sent His Son, born of a woman, born under the Law," and in 3:24 Paul says, "So the Law was our schoolmaster"; the NIV reads "the law was our guardian." Actually, the Greek word *paidagogos* referred to the household slave whose job it was to bring the child to and from school, watch over him, and help raise him correctly in his family. The Law did just that. It kept Israel separate from the nations, made them aware of righteousness and unrighteousness, showed them their need for the mercy of God, and pointed them to the Messiah. Without this preparation, there would have been no salvation for the world, for there would have been no one to receive Jesus Christ as Savior and Lord.

Have you ever wondered what would have happened if Jesus came to India or Africa two thousand years ago? No one would have been waiting for Him. No one would have understood His message. No one would have comprehended the purpose of His death. Even if they had believed in His miracles and His resurrection power, He would have just been added to their almost endless lists of gods. Even if they had acknowledged that He was strong, He would still have been only one of many.

You see, being saved is more than thinking that Jesus the Messiah is great. It is understanding that there is a holy God Whom we have offended, and although our sins against Him have condemned us (and notice that we must have a concept of sin to understand God's judgment and the cross), He has sent His Son to die in our place so that we can have life.

The first apostles could preach this message because God had been preparing them and their forefathers for two thousand years, beginning with Abraham. He had been teaching them the truths of salvation and redemption in types and shadows, so that when the reality came, they would recognize it and follow it. It took fourteen centuries under the law of God to demonstrate to the people of Israel their need for a Savior. It took a gradual unfolding of dozens of prophecies before any of the Jews were ready to receive their heavenly King as a suffering Lamb. Thus, in order for the gospel message to be understood and then proclaimed to the world, the Lord had to have a chosen people. That is why the message came "to the Jews first, and then to the Gentiles" (Romans 1:16).

To tie this in with the subject of our study, let me repeat that in order to keep Israel separated from the world, the greatest battle for the Old Testament men of faith was to get Israel to acknowledge that the Lord alone was God. The one thing that the Israelites did not need to hear was that there was one god who made them sick and another god (in this case with a capital "G") who made them well. The pagan nations were full of their idols who supposedly specialized in sickness and health, death and life, barrenness and fertility, poverty and plenty, calamity and prosperity. The children of Israel had to know that the Lord alone was God, or else they would have been swallowed up by the world.

Let me give you some clear Scriptural examples. If you read them carefully and prayerfully, your light will begin to dawn in dark places.

"I AM THE LORD"

One of the clearest illustrations of this point occurs in the account of the ten plagues inflicted on the Egyptians (Exodus 7:14-12:30). It is important to realize that Egypt had a very crude polytheistic system in which the Pharaoh himself was considered to be a god. Who was this God in whose name Moses spoke so boldly? Where did this Israelite come off demanding that the divine Pharaoh obey the deity of an enslaved people? But God was about to teach the Egyptians a lesson. In fact, in Exodus 9:16 the Lord, speaking through Moses, said these startling words to the ruler of Egypt: "And yet it is for this very purpose that I have kept you alive – so that I might show you My power, and declare My name in all the land." God was going to prove that He alone was the Lord, and that there were no gods besides Him. In Exodus 5:2, Pharaoh said, "Who is the Lord, that I should obey Him? I don't know the Lord and I won't let Israel go!" The Lord replied in 7:5, "The Egyptians will know that I am the Lord when I stretch out My hand upon them and bring My people out from their midst."

When the Lord turned the waters of Egypt into blood, the local magicians duplicated the miracle by their incantations (Exodus 7:20-22). When the second plague was sent and the frogs covered the land, the magicians again were able to produce a similar phenomenon (8:6-7); yet this time Pharaoh requested that Moses pray to the Lord that the land be rid of this plague. Obviously, the Egyptian magicians could get frogs into the land, but not out of it. So, in order to prove to the king that the Lord alone was God (8:10), Moses let Pharaoh set the time that the plague would end, and he then asked God for relief at that very hour. Yet when relief came, Pharaoh hardened his heart (8:15).

By the next plague (namely, the gnats), the magicians couldn't pull another rabbit out of their hats, and they said to Pharaoh, "This is the finger of God" (Exodus 8:19). At least someone was catching on. But Pharaoh wouldn't budge, and so God sent the plague of flies, the plague of boils, and the plague of hail.

Every time Moses spoke in the name of "the Lord, the God of the Hebrews," people must have begun to wonder, "Who is this god? And why can't our gods stop him? Maybe he is the strongest of the gods after all!" Yet God in His mercy was willing to give the Egyptians who feared Him a break. We read in Exodus 9:13-21 that when the Lord sent the plague of hail, He gave advance warning to all the people so that they could protect their cattle and their servants. So, "those officials of Pharaoh who feared the word of the Lord hurried to bring their slaves and their livestock inside. But those who ignored the word of the Lord left their slaves and livestock in the field" (9:20-21, NIV). Although Pharaoh expressed remorse (9:27-28), his heart was still hard (9:35).

Finally, the Lord sent the plague of locusts, and then the plague of darkness. When Pharaoh still refused Moses, this time with the help of divine "hardening" (Exodus 10:27), God carried out the threat which He had made back in Exodus 4:22-23: "This is what the Lord has said: 'Israel is My son, My firstborn. So I say to you (Pharaoh): Send forth My son so that He may worship Me; and if you refuse to send him forth then I am going to kill your son, your firstborn.'" In Exodus 12:12, as the night of the tenth and final plague was approaching, God said, "I will pass through the land of Egypt this very night, and I will strike down all the firstborn in the land of Egypt — from man to beast — and I will bring judgments against all the gods of Egypt. I am the Lord."

Although in Exodus 12:23, God said that when He went through the land to strike down the Egyptians, He would not permit "the destroyer" (Hebrew *haMashkhit*, pron. hah-mash-KHEET) to enter the bloodstained thresholds of the Israelites, it was still He of Whom it was said "at midnight *the LORD* struck down all the firstborn in the land of Egypt" (12:29). In other words, contrary to those who would emphasize the activity of an intermediate agent here, the Lord emphasized that it was *He* Who killed the Egyptian firstborn males (Exodus 4:23, 11:4, 12:12, 29). In Psalm 136:10, the children of Israel were taught to give thanks "to Him Who struck down Egypt's firstborn - for His steadfast love endures forever."

After all this, God had one last display of power for His people. Having miraculously taken them through the Red Sea, He then swept the pursuing Egyptian army under the sea's resurgent waters (Exodus 14:27). When Moses sang to the Lord Who had "hurled the horse and rider into the sea" (Exodus 15:1), he also said with awe and praise, "Who is like You among the gods, O Lord? Who is like You – majestic in holiness, awesome in praise, doing wonders?" (Exodus 15:11; see also Psalm 136:2-4). God had proven His point: there was none like Him in heaven or on earth, all the gods of Egypt were as nothing compared to Him. How frustrating it must have been for the later prophets when the Israelites turned back to Egypt for assistance (see, e.g., Isaiah 30-31).

I have taken some time to develop this point because I want to make one thing clear: to say that God only allowed these plagues to take place, and that He did not bring them about Himself is to seriously misunderstand what the Word is saying. Not to mention the fact that the Bible says the exact opposite of this in the clearest possible language. And what do you think would have happened if Moses had said to Pharaoh, "Listen, king, it's not really our God Who's doing these things to you. It's actually the devil"? Pharaoh would have then asked Moses to get the devil off his back. "Who cares about this Yahweh character anyway? It's the devil who's destroying our land!"

God or the Devil?

Do you see how foolish and impossible this would be? Yet this is what some teachers are saying today. After all, Exodus 15:26, which we discussed in Chapter 1, refers to these very plagues which the Lord put upon the Egyptians. The whole purpose of these punishments was to show Egypt and Israel that the idols who, according to Paul in 1 Corinthians 10:19-20, are actually backed by demonic spirits, were totally powerless and that the Lord alone was God (Exodus 12:12). The last thing God wanted Pharaoh to know was that there was another god named Satan who was pretty strong too.

When we read Exodus 15:10, "You (God) did blow with Your breath [= wind]; the sea covered them," we forget that this was a great statement of faith. In 1400 BC the sea (Hebrew *yam*, pron. YAHM) was considered to be a powerful god in and of itself, and there was another god who was believed to control the wind. Yet God had demonstrated that these "gods" were mere illusions and that all the elements were under His control. Although in ancient Canaanite mythology Leviathan, Yam (= sea), and Mot (= death, pron. MOHT) were all feared as competing and powerful beings, the Israelites acknowledged God alone as the "conqueror" of them all (read carefully Psalms 74:12-17, 89:5-10, 114:1-8; Isaiah 25:7-8, 27:1).

One thing was perfectly clear to this nation of slaves redeemed by the Lord God: whatever angelic forces may have been involved in the ten plagues sent upon Egypt (compare the reference to the destroying angels in Psalms 78:49), it was their Sovereign God Who had sent the plagues, and He alone was responsible. "*He* turned their rivers to blood" (Psalms 78:44); "*He* gave their crops to the grasshopper" (v. 46); "*He* destroyed their vines with hail" (v. 47); "*He* gave over their cattle to the hail" (v. 49); "*He* prepared a path for His anger" (v. 50); "*He* struck down all the firstborn of Egypt" (v. 51; all from NIV). Therefore, to the *Lord alone* belonged the glory and praise (Psalms 78:43 speaks of "the day he displayed His signs in Egypt, His wonders in the region of Zoan," NIV; see also Psalms 136:1-15).

The Philistines Learn a Lesson

Let me give you another example in which it was crucial for a foreign nation to realize that the Lord alone was God and that He ruled over the pagan idols. According to 1 Samuel 4:4-9, after the Philistines had defeated the Israelites in their first battle, they were confronted by a renewed army of Israelites carrying the ark of God into the fray. This put so much fright into the Philistine forces that they cried out, "Woe to us! Who will deliver us from the power of these mighty gods? These are the ones who struck down the Egyptians with every plague in the wilderness" (1 Samuel 4:8). So, with no hope but to fight like men (4:9), they engaged the Israelite army in battle, and, believe it or not, they crushingly defeated them and took the ark of God captive (4:10-11). Apparently, these Israelite gods weren't so strong after all.

Well, it wasn't long before the Philistines found out

that violating the ark of the Lord of heaven and earth wasn't particularly healthy, either for them or for their idols. First, God mocked the chief Philistine god, Dagon (either the god of new grain, compare Hebrew *dagan*, pron. dah-GAHN, "new grain," or the fish god, compare Hebrew *dag*, "fish"; see 1 Samuel 5:1-5). Then, according to 1 Samuel 5:6, "the hand of the Lord was heavy upon the Ashdodites, and He devastated them, striking with hemorrhoids Ashdod and its environs." As the people panicked, they moved the ark around, but the devastation continued (5:7-12).

Finally, after seven months of hemorrhoids, death (1 Samuel 5:11), and rats (6:5), the Philistines consulted with their priests (6:1-9), who instructed them to send the ark back to Israel with a guilt offering for the Lord (6:4-5). They advised them not to harden their hearts against God as Pharaoh and the Egyptians had done (6:6). However, there was to be one test: they were to send the ark back on a cart pulled by two cows, but with no human leaders to direct it. "You watch," said the priests. "If it goes up to its own territory toward Beth Shemesh, then He brought this great calamity upon us; if not, then we will know that His hand did not afflict us; it was just chance" (6:9). Of course, the ark was divinely led back to Israel in the sight of the Philistine rulers (6:10-12), proving to these heathen people that the Lord Yahweh was more powerful than their idols.

What do you think would have happened if some of our faith teachers had been there to talk to the Philistine priests? They would have said, "No, men, it is not God Who has afflicted you. Our God is good; it is Satan who is the thief and the destroyer. If you seek God sincerely to determine who has brought this calamity upon you, then you will find out that it was not the Lord Who did these terrible things." Some of us have correctly spoken these very words to Christians who were under Satanic attack and who mistakenly believed that it was God Who made them sick. And yet, here, in 1 Samuel, according to the clear revelation of God's Word, it was the Lord Who afflicted the Philistines and mocked their god.

You see, Israel had sinned and fallen into divine disfavor, as a result of which they had suffered defeat at the hand of their enemies, even as God had promised (Deuteronomy 28:25). Because of their disobedience, not even the ark could save them. However, if the story had ended at that point, there would have been no more Israel, for, in their eyes, their God would also have suffered defeat. Thus, it was absolutely essential that both the Philistines and Israelites learn that Yahweh alone was God. If the ark did not go back to Israel, then the Philistines would have known that it was by pure chance that they were afflicted. The ark of God, signifying His presence, would have remained in a foreign land and Israel would have had no hope. Their God would have lost the battle. Yet the Lord would not let this happen, for in spite of His people's sin, He would get the glory (see also Ezekiel 36:22-23). So, God proved that He was God in the sight of all the people.

At this point you might say, "Brother, I think you're setting up a straw man. It's totally clear in the Old Testament that God destroyed whole nations for their sin, let alone individuals. Who would deny that He wounded, killed, judged, and afflicted?"

Exactly! Who would possibly deny it except those whose theology found it offensive or wrong? But that is just the problem. I have heard dozens of anointed men and women of God trying to claim that the "original Hebrew" did not mean what it seemed to mean, and that because of certain New Testament truths, the Old Testament truths had to be reinterpreted. Let me categorically state that there is not a single word in any verse which I have quoted regarding God "afflicting," "striking down," "killing," or "destroying" that is capable of a radically different translation. Every verb is active, not passive. God is clearly the working agent, not the helpless onlooker. This is the undisputed verdict of all those who read the Hebrew fluently, and it is the undeniable consensus of every scholarly Hebrew dictionary in any language. But if this still seems hard to accept, then stay with me to the end of this study, and the Spirit of God will give you more than enough truth to replace everything that you may have to discard. *He* will guide us by His Word.

One God Versus Many Gods

As you may know, the Kingdom of Judah was sent into exile in Babylon in 586 BC because of unrepentant sin against their Heavenly King (see 2 Kings 25). Yet the Lord had given prophetic witness through Isaiah and others that the Jewish remnant would return from Babylon and that the idols would be judged (see, e.g., Isaiah 46). God's chosen instrument for this purpose was to be Cyrus, King of Persia, who proclaimed liberty to the captive Jews in 537 BC (see 2 Chronicles 36:23; Ezra 1:1-4) and took the great city of Babylon without a fight (see Isaiah 45:1-3).

Yet there were two problems. First, according to Isaiah 45:4, although God anointed Cyrus, this king did not recognize or know the Lord. The Persian religion, Zoroastrianism, taught an absolute dualism of two almost equally powerful forces, one good and the other evil. Second, while Cyrus gave lip service to Yahweh as God of heaven and earth (see the verses cited above in 2 Chronicles and Ezra), encouraging the Jews to rebuild the temple, he also gave lip service to the other pagan deities, assisting their priests in their temple projects.

In the famous Cyrus Cylinder, written in Babylonian, the Persian king said this: "Marduk [the chief Babylonian god], the great lord . . . ordered him [i.e., Cyrus] to march against his city Babylon . . . I am Cyrus, king of the world . . . whose rule Bel and Nebo love . . . May all the gods whom I have resettled in their sacred cities [and this included Yahweh in Jerusalem] ask daily Bel and Nebo for a long life for me and may they recommend me [to him]; *to Marduk, my lord, they may say this: 'Cyrus, the king who worships you . . .'"* (*Ancient Near Eastern Texts Relating to the Old Testament*, pp. 315-316, my italics).

These facts will help you to understand Isaiah 45:5-7: "I am the Lord, and there is no other; apart from me there is no God. I will strengthen you, though you have not acknowledged me, so that from the rising of the sun to the place of its setting men may know there is none besides me. I am the Lord, and there is no other. I form the light and create darkness, I bring prosperity and create disaster; I, the Lord, do all these things."

Do you see how these verses, especially 45:7, completely undercut the polytheistic views of Cyrus and the other nations? Even God's proclamation that He alone "forms prosperity and creates disaster" totally denies the Zoroastrian dualism ("create" in Hebrew is *bara'*, pron. bah-RAH, used only with God as subject in the Bible).

And here is a glorious truth: although Cyrus may have died in his idolatry, his name and the names of the idols he worshiped are not feared or revered today. Yet the name of the Lord is adored from one end of the earth to the other, and He alone is worshiped as God by untold millions. He brought His people out of Babylon, reestablishing them in their land and teaching them His absolute truth. He prepared them to receive their Messiah and appointed them as the teaching nation. That is why we are saved today. Hallelujah!

Do not be disturbed by the King James translation of Isaiah 45:7 which says, "I create evil." The Hebrew word *ra'* (pron. RAH) can mean "evil," "bad," "calamity," "disaster," or "wrong," depending on the context. Clearly God cannot create moral evil; *ra'* here is the opposite of Hebrew *shalom* (pron. shah-LOHM) meaning "peace," "prosperity," "soundness," or "wholeness." So then, God is taking credit here for bringing peace and prosperity to Cyrus and the Jews but creating calamity and disaster for the Babylonians. He gives light to His people but covers those who oppose Him with darkness.

Thus, our first point in this chapter is that, in contrast to the foreign nations which feared and acknowledged many gods, some of them friendly and others hostile, Israel was to acknowledge the Lord as the one and only true God. We will now develop this point with some further examples in which God is not concerned with Egypt, Philistia, or Persia, but with Israel alone.

THE LORD IS OUR GOD, THE LORD ALONE

We have had occasion to quote Deuteronomy 32:39 several times already: "See now that I myself am He! There is no god besides me. I kill and I make alive. I have wounded and it is I Who heal, and no one can deliver from My hand." Taken alone, it is frightening and grotesque (how do I know that He won't kill me?). But taken in the context of the two main points laid out so far in this chapter and the previous one, it is simple and clear. If you remember the principles of the blessing and the curse, along with the Old Testament emphasis on the Lord alone as God, then this verse will present you with no problems.

The immediate context for Deuteronomy 32, the Song of Moses, actually begins in chapter 27 which lists the curses to be pronounced on Mount Ebal in Canaan. Chapter 28 deals in great detail with the blessings for obedience and the curses for disobedience. In this chapter, as also throughout the book of Deuteronomy, God made it plain that it was His desire to bless His people. Yet if they sinned and followed other gods, they would fall under the curse. Chapter 29 relates Moses's words to the new generation born in the wilderness as he publicly renews the covenant with them. In chapter 30 he sets before them the offer of life and death, blessing and curse. Then, after Joshua is announced as Moses's successor in 31:1-7, Moses and Joshua are summoned by the Lord to the Tent of Meeting. There God tells Moses, "You are about to lie down with your fathers, and this people will arise and fornicate after the foreign gods of the land which they are entering. They will forsake Me and nullify My covenant which I made with them . . . . Now, write for yourselves this song and teach it to the children of Israel and put it in their mouths, so that this song will be a witness for Me *against* the children of Israel" (29:16, 19; see also 29:19-28; 31:21: "and it shall come to pass, when all these great calamities and sorrows overtake them then this song will testify against them . . .").

Therefore, in the context of Deuteronomy 27-31, chapter 32 stood as a song of witness to rebuke apostate Israel for their sin and to call them to repentance. They had worshiped other gods but now found that these idols were powerless. They had learned firsthand that Yahweh had wounded and put to death. Now He was saying to them, "Turn back to Me! For although I have wounded, it is My desire to heal; though it is I Who killed, it is My will to make you alive." Once again, He was offering total restoration to those who would repent.

Israel Learns a Lesson

In the history of Israel, the covenant nation often went whoring after other gods (see, e.g., Jeremiah 2; Ezekiel 16; and especially Hosea 1:2, 2:2-13, 4:10-19, 5:1-7, 6:10, 7:4-8, 9:1, 11:2, 13:1-3), thus falling under the curse. Blinded by their sin, they did not initially recognize that it was the Lord Who was withholding His blessings (Hosea 2:8). In fact, according to Amos 4:6-11, even after God sent famine and plague upon His disobedient people, they still did not return to Him. Judgment fell heavily in 722 BC, and Israel learned that Assyria, in whom it had been trusting, could not save or heal (Hosea 5:13), but only destroy. The sinful nation had, by their rebellion, challenged the divine Lion, and they now lay helplessly ripped and torn.

Yet the revelation of the Word was beginning to give them light. Israel and Judah saw that their only hope was in God. "Assyria will not save us. On (war) horses we will not ride. Never again will we say 'our gods' to the work of our hands – for in You the orphan finds mercy" (Hosea 14:3; contrast 13:16). The divine response is a glorious example of God's tender compassion: "I will heal their backslidings; I will love them freely, for My anger has turned away from them" (Hosea 14:3). He Who said, "I will slay their cherished offspring," now took great delight in saying, "I will be like the dew to Israel" (14:4).

Praise God!

The mercy and grace of the Father of compassion had been poured out upon this wandering nation of sheep who had finally returned to the sheepfold. But when did the turning point take place? It was in Hosea 6:1, when Deuteronomy 32:39 became living truth in the heart of the people, and with one voice they exclaimed, "Come, and let us turn back to the Lord; for it is He Who has torn, but He will heal us; He struck down, but He will bind us up." These words, Israel's biblical confession of faith, were not based on ignorance, but on revelation. They had rightly apprehended the dealings of their faithful God.

Now I ask you, in Hosea's own words (Hosea 14:9): Are you wise? Do you understand these things? "For the Lord's ways are right, and the righteous walk in them; but the rebellious stumble in them." One God, one revelation, one purpose; yet to those who oppose Him, and thereby commit spiritual suicide, He is like a lion. To those who call on Him in truth, He is like the dew. To lean on worthless idols is to incur His wrath; to trust only in Him is to receive His mercy.

Some scholars have suggested that Hosea's repeated usage of the Hebrew root *rapha'* (Hosea 5:13, 6:1, 7:1, 11:3, 14:5) is explained by the fact that one of the key false gods that Israel worshiped was a "healer god."

(Most of the important gods in the ancient pagan world, as well as in today's unchristianized lands, were believed to have healing powers.) If this is true, which in all probability it is, then it is plain to see that the chosen people had to learn for themselves that one God, and one God alone, had the power to wound and, more importantly, the power to heal.

When the fullness of time had come, the Lord could clearly reveal to us that there was an infinitely inferior being named Satan who was directly associated with sickness and disease. But for the purpose of having a monotheistic nation prepared to receive their Messiah and then teach the world, it was necessary in the Old Testament to limit the direct number of references to this enemy of our souls. He was to be viewed as God's agent for destruction, with the emphasis being on the supremacy of the Lord and His will, and the subservience of all creation to Him.

Nebuchadnezzar My Servant

If this still startles you, let me remind you of some Old Testament truths. In Jeremiah 27:6, God called Nebuchadnezzar "My servant," even though this Babylonian king committed all kinds of atrocities against the Jewish people. Yet the Lord was demonstrating to the world that the gods of Babylon had not triumphed over the God of Israel; rather Nebuchadnezzar himself was only a pawn in Yahweh's hand. However, even this king was to be judged for his pride, cruelty, and idolatry (see Daniel 4:1-37; I suggest at this point that you read carefully Isaiah 10:5-34 in the light of Isaiah 36 and 37).

First Kings 22 gives us another example of God using a fallen spirit for His purpose. The true prophet Michaiah, hated by the Israelite king for his uncompromising words (22:8), was called upon by the king of Judah to speak from the Lord (see 22:1-7). When he finally told the whole story, totally contradicting the false assurance of the lying prophets, he recounted this vision: "I saw the Lord sitting on his throne with all the army of heaven standing by Him, to His right and to His left. And the Lord said, 'Who will entice Ahab so that he will go up and fall in Ramoth Gilead?' And one said this, and another said that. Then one spirit came out, stood before the Lord, and said, 'I will go out and I will be a lying spirit in the mouths of all his (i.e., Ahab's) prophets.' So He said, 'You will entice him, and you will prevail. Go out, and do so.' Now, then, see that the Lord has put a lying spirit in the mouths of these prophets of yours, for He has decreed disaster for you" (vv. 19-23).

Habakkuk 3 sheds even more light on this subject, but

only when studied in the Hebrew. In the NIV, Habakkuk 3:3-5 reads like this: "God came from Teman, the Holy One from Mount Paran. Selah . . . His splendor was like the sunrise; rays flashed from his hand, where his power was hidden. *Plague* went before him; *pestilence* followed His steps" (my italics). Now, this is important because the Hebrew word used for pestilence was *resheph* (pron. REH-sheph), and this "Resheph" was well known in the land of Canaan – he was the famous god of pestilence! Yet in the Old Testament revelation, he was no divine being at all; he was only a thing, a non-entity, totally under Yahweh's control.

Again, I must emphasize here as I did in the previous chapter, that this does not teach us that the Lord used to put sickness on his faithful children. It only teaches us that all the elements of this world were under His control. They were not part of an equally powerful opposing kingdom. God asked the slow-tongued Moses this rhetorical question: "Who made man's mouth? Or who makes deaf people, or dumb, or seeing, or blind? Isn't it I, the Lord?" (Exodus 4:11). However, and this is important, He was not saying to him, "Tough luck Moses! I made you stutter because that's My lasting plan for your life." No, He was saying, "Moses, why are you so faithless? Who do you think made you anyway? Who do you think created everything there is? It was Me, Moses, your God. So don't you think that I can correct your speech?" (Read

v. 12: "Now then, go! And I will be with your mouth and will teach you what to speak.") Once more, God was revealing Himself as the Healer of His people.

If you ask me whether or not the ancient pagan nations weren't right after all in attributing sickness and disease to various demons and gods, I would say that they were more wrong than right, for their understanding of the spiritual realm was almost totally false. They did not know that there was only one true God and Lord, Creator of all. Instead, they believed in many gods, gods who were often immoral, bloodthirsty, capricious, moody, and irritable. In this view demons even inhabited rocks and trees, and the sun, moon, and stars were all considered gods. According to the Babylonian account of creation, heaven and earth were formed when the young god Marduk split the goddess Tiamat in half and mixed part of her with the defeated sea god, Apsu. In one Egyptian story of creation, the male god Atum, having no female to impregnate, produced his own seed (i.e., self-procreation, to put it nicely). From this seed, the other gods were born.

Thus, it is clear that whatever these peoples believed about demonic activity, it was not learned by revelation but rather by satanic superstitions and traditions. Therefore, in not denying the existence of such beings (or other angelic beings; compare Psalm 29:1, 89:5-8), but instead in asserting Yahweh's supremacy and rule over all, the Old Testament revelation was completely true. What happened in the New Testament is that God lifted the curtain on the spiritual world and declared release to the prisoners, triumphing over sin and the devil in the Messiah's cross (Colossians 2:15). He then committed His authority to the Church, and through us His Kingdom goes forth in power, crushing Satan under our feet (Luke 10:19; see Chapter 5 for the whole glorious picture).

And would you like to know what the children of Israel did to the one "intermediate agent" of healing used supernaturally by God in the Old Testament, namely, the bronze snake? According to Numbers 21:4-9, because the people spoke against God and Moses, the Lord sent venomous snakes among them, and many people died of the bites. When they repented, Moses was told by the Lord to make a bronze snake and put it on a pole. Whoever was bitten could then look at it and live. So, what did the later generations do to this powerless piece of bronze? They burned incense to it, that's what! (See 2 Kings 18:4; they even gave it a name!)

So then, have we demonstrated our point clearly, beyond any reasonable doubt? Understand, then, that in order for us to be saved today, there had to be a people with the revelation of God in their hands. And for this people to be preserved in the midst of perverse idolatry, they had to know that their God, and their God alone, was Lord and King of all. When it was time for the plan of redemption to be revealed, it was revealed to Paul the Jew. And it was revealed by means of the Old Testament Scripture (Romans 16:25-26: "So that all nations might believe and obey him.") Without the chosen nation and their Bible, the world would never have known God. Amazing, but true. The eternal Son entered this world as a Jew.

"Oh, the depth of the riches of the wisdom and knowledge of God! How unsearchable His judgments, and His paths beyond tracing out!" (Romans 11:33). "Oh, the depth of the riches of the wisdom and knowledge of God! How unsearchable His judgments, and His paths beyond tracing out!" (Romans 11:33).

HE WILL TURN OUR STUMBLING BLOCKS INTO STEPPING STONES

CHAPTER 4

THE LESSON OF THE BOOK OF JOB

When the prophet Samuel was a little boy serving at the tabernacle in Shiloh, the Lord tried to speak to him in the middle of the night. Each time God called "Samuel, Samuel," the young boy ran to Eli the priest saying, "Here I am, for you called me." Samuel said this because at that time he "did not yet recognize the Lord, and the word of the Lord had not yet been revealed to him" (1 Samuel 3:7). But after this happened three times, Eli realized that it was the voice of God, and he gave Samuel this wise advice: "Go lie down; and if He calls you, then say, 'Speak Lord, for your servant is listening'" (1 Samuel 3:9).

Any time God speaks to us, we ought to listen. And when the Lord takes forty-two chapters of His precious Word to tell us something, we better listen carefully. He did not give us a book covering more pages than half of Paul's letters put together so as to create problems for us. He gave us the book of Job because He had something important to say. He did not allow His faithful servant to suffer such pain and agony so that we could poke fun at him and judge him. Rather, the Lord permitted one of His most devoted children to pass through a fiery trial in order that many might gain understanding from his experience. If we learn the lesson of the book of Job (and I don't mean just chapters 1-2 and 42; the whole book is important), then our lives will be fuller, our understanding deeper, *and our faith stronger.*

Let us begin by looking at the only verses in the Bible outside of the book of Job which speak of this man: "And the word of the Lord came to me saying, 'Son of man, if a country sins against Me by committing treachery, and I stretch forth My hand against it, destroying its supply of food, and I send famine in it and cut off from it man and beast — if these three men were in her midst, Noah, Daniel, and Job, they would only save themselves by their righteousness, declares the Lord Yahweh'" (Ezekiel 14:12-14; see also 14:20); "Brothers, as an example of patience in the face of suffering, take the prophets who spoke in the name of the Lord. As you know, *we consider blessed those who have persevered.* You have heard of Job's perseverance and have seen what the Lord finally brought about. The Lord is full of compassion and mercy" (James 5:10-11, my italics).

THE JOB OF THE BIBLE

These are not the descriptions of a man who married the wrong woman, walked in ignorance, and operated in fear. God Himself said that there was no one like him on earth. The Job who is described by many of today's faith teachers is anything but a hero of righteousness, faith, and perseverance. He makes all the wrong confessions, prays the wrong prayers, and opens the door wide for the enemy to come right in. Thank God, the Job of much of our contemporary preaching is not the Job of the Bible!

According to the Lord's Word in Ezekiel, Job was an almost legendary figure of righteousness, in the ranks of Noah and Daniel. If anyone had a right to divine preservation it was this man (read again Ezekiel 14:12-20). According to James, Job was a great example of perseverance in the face of suffering. He hung in there until the Lord brought about his deliverance.

Now, please forgive me if I seem blunt, but if your opinion of Job is different from this, then you have an unbiblical view of this man of God. The description of Job in

Chapter 1 of his book is that of an ideal righteous man enjoying the blessing of God. He was upright, rich, and conscientious. Do all of us live as he did — truthful in our dealings, faithful to our wives, just toward our workers, feeding the hungry, clothing the poor, sheltering the homeless, always trusting God and never trusting our possessions (Job 31:1-40)? He was an exemplary man of faith, and God plainly told Satan that there was no cause for Job to be afflicted (2:3). The devil could not touch him unless the Lord allowed it (1:10-11). That is why Satan had to seek His permission. When God said, "Behold, all that he has is in your power; only don't touch *him*" (1:12), He was prescribing the limits within which Satan could operate. If the door was already open, the devil would not have had to argue with God; he could have simply attacked at will. As it is, Satan couldn't touch Job's body until he received permission (1:12 and 2:6). Even then he was still not allowed to kill him (2:6).

We pointed out in Chapter 1 that Job was in no way "operating in fear," and again we would emphasize that, according to the Scriptures, Job feared God and not man or unforeseen calamities. Verse 26 of Job chapter 3 does not contradict this. Either it should be translated in the past tense, "I wasn't complacent, or quiet, or resting, and yet agony came" (in other words, I hadn't fallen asleep under the blessings of God, but I was alert and on guard, yet calamity struck unexpectedly), or we could translate with the NIV in the present tense, "I have no peace, no quietness; I have no rest, but only turmoil" (i.e., because of my affliction I am in great anguish. In that case, we should translate 3:25 in the present tense as well: "For what I fear comes upon me, and what I dread overtakes me").

Because I recognize that many of you reading this have been taught to the contrary, I want to help you with a powerful example from 1980s. But first notice that Job 1:4-5 does not state that Job's children were guilty of riotous carousing; only that they regularly feasted together as a family. If they had been wild and ungodly, then they certainly would not have allowed their father to constantly have them purified (Job 1:5; on purification see Exodus 19:10,14; Joshua 3:5, 7:13; 1 Samuel 16:5). Job interceded for them just in case they sinned in their hearts (i.e., in their thoughts) against God. In the midst of an enjoyable party, it is not impossible for young people to allow an ungodly thought to fester and grow in their minds. Therefore, as a godly father, Job offered sacrifices for his children. However, it is commonly taught in some faith circles that Job ought to have believed that his children would not sin, and therefore his intercession was really anti-faith (i.e., fear motivated). Seriously!

STANDING IN THE GAP

What do we say then of the testimony of a young evangelist, a man whose grandfather was a famous and respected evangelist who faithfully served God for decades and whose father was a serious, committed believer? Beginning in the early 1980s, this young man was being used prominently in ministry around the world, yet he will freely admit that there was a time in his life when he ran from God and His call, falling headlong into sin.

Now, my point is that if there was a vulnerable time in the life of this fine Christian even though he was raised in the faith, is it so peculiar to think that there may have been a time of vulnerability in the lives of Job's children? And could not the Spirit of God have moved upon Job to "stand in the gap" for his children, who had been blessed and who might have taken the Lord for granted? (Note Proverbs 30:8-9: "Two things I have asked of You. Do not withhold them from me before I die. Remove vanity and falsehood far from me, and neither poverty nor riches give me, but only apportion me my daily bread. Lest I be satisfied and deny [You] saying, 'Who is the Lord?'")

COMING TO JOB'S DEFENSE

Am I trying to defend Job? Absolutely. He has had more than his share of "worthless comforters" (Job 16:2). It is time for the Church of Christ to stop finding fault with this righteous servant whom God commended and to cease from inventing causes for his sufferings. The whole point of Job 1 and 2 is that, according to everything Job and his friends knew and believed, there was no possible way such calamities could come upon a godly man like himself. On the wicked, yes, but on the righteous, impossible. (If you are not familiar with Psalm 73, I suggest that you read it now. There the psalmist wrestles with the other side of our question, namely, "Why do the wicked prosper?")

Job's friends, unwilling to bend in their beliefs (and, by and large, their basic beliefs were right) had two choices before them: either Job was guilty of some unknown secret sin, or he was an exception to everything they knew about God and His ways. Since they could not believe that the latter possibility was true then, in their minds, the calamities which befell Job were the natural consequences of a hitherto hidden transgression. Thus, little by little, they became convinced that Job had better repent and get right with God.

In Job 5:18, Eliphaz encourages Job to receive God's chastening in love, "for He has caused pain, but He will bind up; His hands have struck down, but they will heal" (5:18). Yet this quotation, which sounds like Deuteronomy 32:39 and Hosea 6:1, was the wrong word at the wrong time, for, *contrary to sinful Israel, Job had done nothing to merit the curse.* No one knew that behind the scenes a malicious spirit had received permission to test God's servant (compare Luke 22:31), and therefore Job's sufferings were not brought about by his sin, nor were they brought about by his supposed ignorance or fear. As one commentator noted, Job was not afflicted because of his sin; rather, he sinned because of his affliction, lashing out at God in the midst of His pain, provoked by the words of his friends.

Ultimately, Job never found out that it was the devil who caused his anguish. That was not part of the revelation which God gave him in Job chapters 38-41. In accordance with the Old Testament revelation, Job believed that it was the Lord Who gave and the Lord Who took away (see the previous chapter). When he repented of foolish talk in Job 40:3-5 and 42:1-6, it was the speeches of chapters 3-31 that he was renouncing. In those chapters he justified himself, challenged God, and accused Him of making a mockery of justice. But when he said that God took away, he did not sin or attribute to the Lord anything out of character (1:22; see the discussion of this verse in chapter 1). At that point in his life, Job was going to trust God regardless of what he saw or experienced; that is faith! The prophet Habakkuk made a similar determination: "Though the fig tree does not bud and there are no grapes on the vines, though the olive crop fails and the fields produce no food, though there are no sheep in the pen and no cattle in the stalls, yet I will rejoice in the Lord, I will be joyful in God my Savior" (Habakkuk 3:17-18, NIV).

I am not saying, however, that we should confess today that "the Lord gave and the Lord took away" if the devil rips us off. If we can see clearly that Satan has robbed us, why would we say, "The Lord took away"? Instead, it was the devil who acted like a thief and robber and murderer (see John 8:44; 10:10). Yet from Job's perspective he was speaking in great faith, not ignorance (and, to be sure, there are times when the Lord does take certain things away from us, but always for our lasting good). Also, we should not judge all saints who quote Job 1:21 today. Maria Woodworth-Etter recited Job 1:21 when her son Willie died at the age of seven, and she was certainly an anointed woman of faith and power. Aimee Semple MacPherson even said that the Spirit of God rose within her when her husband Robert Semple died at a young age, causing her to say, "The Lord gave and the Lord took away." So, let's not be so quick to judge and criticize. Just because someone doesn't have the same perspective you do doesn't make them unspiritual.

James reminds us of the latter end of Job: "You . . . have seen what the Lord finally brought about" (James 5:11). If we jump to the last chapter of the Book of Job, we see that the "orthodox faith theology" is thoroughly substantiated. Job's body is healed, his friends return, he has ten more blessed children, God gives him twice as much material wealth as he had before, and he lives long and prospers (Job 42:10-17).

So if the "final end" of Job is just what we would expect, then the problems associated with this book must be those presented in the previous chapters of Job: 1) why do the righteous sometimes suffer inexplicably; 2) what do we do when the Word apparently hasn't worked and our faith has been temporarily shattered; and 3) how do the trials of Job apply to us today?

The answers to these questions and the resultant lessons learned will be developed in what follows. But first let me give you a very moving story as recounted by an international teacher speaking to over eight thousand believers in the summer of 1983.

Having related the divine call to minister internationally with his singing group, this brother then described the group's successful work in Africa, Europe, and especially behind the Iron Curtain. This was over a period of several years, up until the fall of 1982. Then while working in England, he was given a piece of unbelievable news: his precious wife had been killed in an automobile accident in the States, and now he was left a widower with three children.

Naturally, he was totally crushed by this report and returned home broken. How could it be that he gave himself completely to the work of the Lord, only to have something like this happen in his family? In his anguish, he went to see the most prominent faith teacher of the day who spoke these precious words to him: "Son, there are some things we just simply will never understand, and there are no answers for them." But, he added, "You can't lose your grip in God." This, in a nutshell, is the message of the Book of Job. When all else fails, don't lose your grip in God. Heaven and earth will pass away, but God remains faithful still. And, so as not to leave out the end of the story, just as God in the end restored the fortunes of Job, so this brother's ministry subsequently took on absolutely supernatural proportions. Hallelujah!

A FUTURE HOPE

Thus, the first important lesson to be learned from a study of Job is this: Sometimes inexplicable events may transpire which totally contradict everything you have been taught to expect. Hang in there, for your expected end will come, either in this world or the world to come (Proverbs 23:18; see also Psalm 37:73). If you have received the exact opposite of that for which you exercised faith, don't give up. The Lord will yet come through.

The Hebrew word for "final end" is *'akharit* (pron. a-kha-REET, literally, "that which comes after"), and it plays an important role in Old Testament thought. The whole purpose of God's wisdom is "that you may be wise in your final *end*" (Proverbs 19:20 — "your *'akharit*"). We are warned to look out for the adulterous woman, for her final *end* is death (Proverbs 5:3-23, 6:24-35, 7:1-27). Also, although alcohol may seem sweet to the taste, in the *end* it bites like a viper (Proverbs 23:32). As for the wicked, their final *end* is destruction (Proverbs 14:12), and their hope is cut off (Psalms 37:38, 109:13). In fact, Proverbs says that the wicked don't even have an *'akharit* - i.e., their expected end is empty, for they shall have darkness, and not light (see Proverbs 24:20). But the righteous have a blessed future (Jeremiah 29:11; Proverbs 23:18, 24:14; Psalm 37:37: "there is an *'akharit* for the man of peace"). We have an expected end. God will richly reward us for our faith in Him.

Now here is an important point. The Old Testament "future hope" was primarily "this world" oriented. The blessing of God was seen almost exclusively in terms of earthly success and exaltation of the righteous. The godly lived on, in a sense, in their offspring (Isaiah 38:18-19; Psalm 22:30-31), and the answers to human suffering were looked for mainly in this life. But our hope as New Testament believers clearly reaches into eternity, and, in fact, at the moment of our new birth, we took on the eternal life of God. Therefore, the "this world" answer of Job 42 is only a starting point for the Christian. The day will come before the throne of our God when, enveloped in His love and light, we will receive back again a billion times over everything of ours that Satan has ever touched. And, although we need not wait for that day to "reclaim" the land, we must remember that for some the full payback cannot come till then. For Job, his test in full intensity was only for a moment; his full reward was soon to come.

A Problem for Theology

Job's friends couldn't understand this; it contradicted their theology. But let's face it. Job's sufferings contradict a lot of some of our theology too. Otherwise, we wouldn't be inventing causes for his afflictions. Isn't it the truth? If we hear of some tragedy wherein a Christian family is killed in a plane crash, some of us immediately judge their faith and walks with the Lord. The Book of Job tells us to keep quiet. Maybe we are right, and the disaster could have been prevented. But maybe there's something going on that we don't understand. Of course, we won't blame God; the Book of Job teaches us that too. But let's learn to keep our mouths shut and hold up the afflicted in prayer.

You see, in and of themselves, separated from the context of Job's sufferings, the speeches of his friends were, for the most part, biblically correct (read, for example, Job 5:11-27 and compare it with Psalm 91; it sounds good, doesn't it?). Yet we have no business throwing our orthodox judgments on an afflicted saint. "Well, if you had enough faith, your husband wouldn't have died," or, "If this had been so-and-so, he wouldn't have let the devil do that to his family," or, "See, I told you, you weren't living right." But that is what Job's comforters did, and it is exactly what we do today. "You see, Job was walking in fear," or, "Poor guy, look at what he got for a wife," or, "See what happens when you live in ignorance?" God actually rebuked Job's friends for not speaking rightly of Him, as Job had done (see Job 42:7-9). God would rather have us be honest with Him than spout out empty theological maxims learned from man.

"I Am That I Am"

Job chapters 1-2 teach us that there are sometimes unseen factors (as in Daniel 10:12-14) which can temporarily cause unexpected results. At such times, we had better use our high-powered faith confessions against the enemy's attacks and not against our suffering brother. But let me also mention that, from our vantage point, Job 1 and 2 make it clear that the Lord did not stretch out his hand to destroy; every time Satan said, "Stretch out your hand" to God, the Lord replied, "You go and do it" (Job 1:11-12, 2:5-6). Thus, God was clearly not the direct author of Job's sufferings. But here is something important: when the Lord spoke to Job out of the whirlwind in chapters 38-41, He did not say a word about Job's sufferings, nor did he mention anything about the devil. *He only revealed Himself.* And that was sufficient. When Job saw the eternal God in His wisdom, power, and beauty, he repented of his defiance (see e.g., Job 9:22-24, 10:13-17, 16:7-14), humbling himself before the Lord of the universe. The basic answer of the Book of Job is simply this: God is.

If we look again to Job 42, we are presented with a further answer to our questions, for in the end what Satan meant for evil, God used for good. This is also the lesson of the sufferings of Joseph; what his brothers meant for death, God used for life (see especially Genesis 45:4-7).

Ultimately this is also the lesson of the cross. The most grotesque crime committed in the history of the world – the crucifixion of the sinless Son of God – is the very tool used by God to save the lost. Joseph, Job, and Jesus. Look at them carefully, for their final ends were blessed.

The Bible is totally clear on this point. The trying of our faith produces perseverance, perseverance character, and character hope (see Romans 5:3-4; James 1:2-4; see also James 1:12; 1 Peter 4:12). In the midst of Job's anguish, look at how his crying out began to develop into confident assurance in God. First, there is a wish uttered in desperation: "If only there were someone to arbitrate between us, to lay his hand upon us both, someone to remove God's rod from me, so that His terror would frighten me no more. Then I would speak without fear of Him, but as it now stands with me, I cannot" (Job 9:33-35, NIV). Then, there comes the beginning of faith: "Earth, do not cover my blood; may my cry never be laid to rest! Even now my witness is in heaven; my advocate is on high. My intercessor is my friend as my eyes pour out tears to God; on behalf of a man he pleads with God as a man pleads for his friend" (16:18-21, NIV). Then comes an explosion of faith: "I know that My Redeemer lives, and that in the end He will stand upon the earth. And after my skin has been destroyed, yet in my flesh I will see God; I myself will see Him with my own eyes — I, and not another. How my heart yearns within me!" (19:25-27,

NIV). Oh, what a confession! *This man had faith.*

Add to all this one more blessing. As a result of his suffering, Job could now say to God, "I had heard of You by the hearing of the ear; but now my eye sees You" (Job 42:5). Having passed through the fire he had met the living God in truth. Doesn't this remind you of Paul's heart cry in Philippians 3:10-11? "I want to know Christ and the power of his resurrection and the fellowship of sharing in His sufferings, becoming like Him in His death, and so, somehow, to attain to the resurrection of the dead."

Did God Use Sickness?

Before anyone misunderstands me, I am not stating that God uses sickness to discipline His children, nor am I saying that being sick is "sharing in Christ's sufferings." I am only saying that if we are walking with the Lord, whatever the devil throws in our path can be turned around for God's glory and our growth. Although some Greek manuscripts of Romans 8:28 say, "And we know that all things work together for good to them that love God, to them who are called according to *his* purpose" (so KJV), other manuscripts read, "And we know that in all things God works for the good of those who love Him, who have been called according to His purpose" (so NIV). There is a big difference here. All things, in and of themselves, do not work for our good; this is clear. But *in all things* our God is actively working for our good. And if we cooperate with Him, then as one Christian song proclaimed, "He will turn our stumbling blocks into stepping stones."

PERSEVERANCE IN GOD

I want to point out something else in Job which deserves our attention. When everything else failed and all hope was lost, Job took his refuge in God. He ran away from the God who he thought was out to get him, but he fled into the arms of the God Who could save him. It sounds like a paradox, but how many times have we lived there ourselves? When our faith has disappointed us, what is the answer? Faith! When it seems that the Word has let us down, where do we turn? To the Word! When it looks like Jesus just hasn't come through and our lives are hopelessly crushed, on Whose name do we call? Jesus! The Book of Job tells us that we may, in fact, lose ourselves for a while when the skies look black. But when we finish our faithless wrangling and complaining, God tells us to humble ourselves and turn back. He is still there waiting. Truly, God is good.

For those seeking a simple solution, the Book of Job provides that also, on a certain level (in reality, the book of Job is too magnificent to put in a little box of spiritual formulas). In the end Job lives long and prospers, receiving healing for his body, ten more children, twice as many possessions, and reinstatement of his social status (Job 42:10-17). But what do we tell those whose lives are lost somewhere in the middle chapters of Job's despair (e.g., Job chapters 3, 7, or 14)? What do we tell those who have suffered for years, without relief?

We remember to be compassionate rather than being like Job's comforters, who were more concerned to justify their beliefs than to help a brother in need. What if his faith did fail for a while and he did get a little out of line in his anger? If he wasn't such a man of character, he would have totally cursed God and never come back. His integrity held him in place.

Really now, some of us get a cold and start complaining if it doesn't disappear instantly. "Oh Lord, I thought You loved me. But now You've let me down." Isn't that what we say? We can't pay our cell phone bill, and we wonder if God's promises are really true.

Not Job. This man had guts. He had a supernatural stick-to-it-tiveness. After all his calamities, he was still worshiping God ("May the name of the Lord be praised"; end of Job 1:21). Yet his friends centered in on his obvious faults, and when that didn't work, they made up a few of their own. Their theology had become for them a straitjacket. When Jesus confronted the similarly bound religious leaders of His day, He told them, "Go and learn what this means: 'I desire mercy, not sacrifice'" (Matthew 8:13). Let's make sure that we learn that lesson first. Then we can go and give light to the afflicted.

The Best is Yet to Come

But what do we tell those suffering if God's answer seems so distant and faint? Tell them this: God remains faithful, even when our circumstances tell us the opposite, and the final end of the righteous is always blessed. Minister to them according to their faith, and build them up to receive again from the Lord. Bring them assurance that their God is good – perfectly good. And even if, according to all outward appearances, the Lord's promises have failed, turn their hearts back to God. That is the essence of faith. Tell them to look, not at what they can see, but at what they can't see (2 Corinthians 4:16-18). Take hold of their hearts and minds, and don't let them go.

One healing evangelist said that on certain occasions, he paid for sick people to go the doctor. Why was this? Simply because he knew that in their present state of faith and knowledge, they would not receive miraculous healing. We can learn a similar lesson. Although the ending of the Book of Job totally strongly supports a message of faith and healing, we should not force it upon a sufferer whose faith is weak. Meet him where he is. If all he can hear is that heaven is waiting for him when he dies, then tell him that. Maybe little by little you can show him that his answer can come sooner than he thinks. And when your spirits join together in faith, take hold of God. The promise will then find its way to you.

Remember, "We consider blessed those who have persevered" (James 5:11). "Blessed is the man who perseveres under trial, because when he has stood the test, he will receive the crown of life that God has promised to those who love him" (James 1:12). "Therefore, among God's churches we boast about your perseverance and faith in all the persecutions and trials you are enduring" (2 Thessalonians 1:4). To the afflicted saint, the word from God is always sure. Hang in there, for help is on the way. In fact, if you look good and hard, you'll see that the Helper has never left you. Somewhere, somehow, He has left you tokens of His grace.

In the midst of his sufferings, it seemed impossible to Job that God could ever truly restore all he had lost. After all, he suffered the loss of his children as well as his health and possessions. Did the fact that Job received ten more children really make up for the fact that his first ten were gone? But it is here that we have another key point, for there is a hint of future hope in Job 42:12-15. Although Job received back twice as much as he had before in material possessions, he only had ten more children, not twenty. *The first ten were waiting for him on the other side.* Therefore, what we can't get back in this present world, we will get back in glory. There is nothing the enemy steals that the believer can't reclaim, for all things are ours (1 Corinthians 3:22). There is always hope for the believer.

Although I have much more to say about the Book of Job (for which I highly recommend my commentary), I need to bring my thoughts to a close. There are only two more things that I believe God would have us consider.

COUNTING THE COST

Job's sufferings force the question, "Would I be willing to serve God if I lost everything? Would I serve Him just because He's God?" Jesus said to those who would follow Him, "Count the cost. If you don't give up everything you have, you can't be My disciple" (see Luke 14:28-33). The famous "hundredfold blessing" was promised to those who left all and followed the Lord (Mark 10:28-30). Job said that no matter what it took, he would follow God. (The very basis of Satan's accusation was that Job was only serving God for the blessings [Job 1:9-10] and that if the Lord took them away, he would curse Him to His face. And Satan tempted Jesus by offering Him all the kingdoms of the world if He would only bow down and worship him.)

In one great moment of faith, Job spoke these well-known words: "Even if He kills me, I'll yet hope in Him" (Job 13:15). Could we have said the same thing if we stood in his shoes? Granted, God is not going to kill us. But would we follow Him if He said to us, "Sell your possessions and give to the poor" (Luke 12:33)? Or do we follow Him only for the fishes and the loaves? The Book of Job makes us ask ourselves these very things. Rather than us pointing the finger at Job, I think that, in a sense, he's pointing the finger at us.

The "fiery trial" (1 Peter 4:12) is not always pleasant. Persecution does not feel good on the flesh (ask Paul if you don't believe me). The heroes of faith didn't always have it easy (read Hebrews 11:32-37 concerning exploits of men and women of faith). Are we willing to pass through the purifying flames so that, by them, we might grow up into the full stature of Christ? "For it has been granted to you on behalf of Christ not only to believe on Him, but also to suffer for Him" (Philippians 1:29). The apostles rejoiced "because they had been counted worthy of suffering disgrace for the Name" (Acts 5:41). Would we count ourselves blessed if we were called on to suffer?

PERSECUTION OR SICKNESS?

If your first reaction is, "Persecution, yes; sickness, no," then I would agree with you. But remember that although Job did not suffer persecution *per se* (except, in a sense, from his friends), he did suffer satanic attack because of his faith (see also 1 Peter 5:8-10). I do not know why Smith Wigglesworth went through six years of physical agony, passing hundreds of kidney stones out of his body while he stood firmly upon the Word. During that time, his public miracle ministry impacted the nations. But in his own life there was an intense struggle taking place, yet a struggle from which he emerged in greater faith and power. Peter said that sometimes, "for a little while," we may "suffer grief in all kinds of trials." But "these have come so that your faith — of greater worth than gold, which perishes even though refined by fire — may be proved genuine and may result in praise, glory and honor when Jesus Christ is revealed" (1 Peter 1:6-7).

Thus, there is an important lesson to be learned here. While being sick, in and of itself, is absolutely not "suffering for the Lord," standing upon the Word in the midst of satanic attack definitely carries with it a measure of suffering for Jesus. When we say to the devil, "No sir! I'm not going to take what you are trying to give me, for the Word is true. I'm not going to crawl into my sick bed and give up. No way! I resist you Satan in the name of the Lord," we are entering right into the battle fray, and it takes determination to press through. Although there may be temporary setbacks, we do not quit.

The Promises of God

This brings us to our last question regarding the Book of Job. How does this story line up with our present position in Jesus? Does the enemy have access to us in the same way he had access to Job? According to the Word the answer is no, definitely not. Jesus has destroyed the works of the evil one (1 John 3:8). He spoiled principalities and powers in the cross (Colossians 2:15), and He has been given as the head over all things to the Church (Ephesians 1:22). "Lord, even the demons submit to us in your name" (Luke 10:17). Therefore, we need not fear the work of the enemy, for sudden disaster shall not overtake us (Psalm 91:3-10; see Chapter 5 for more on this subject).

Yet the application of Job is simple. Even though we have these promises and we are not in bondage to fear (remember, Job may have had some of these promises too, although not a fraction of what we now possess), there are still some inexplicable events which may confront us. My first forty-seven years with the Lord have at times seemed like a fairy tale, with God just pouring in blessing upon blessing. It seems that almost everything I put my hand to is blessed, and I suffer no real lack in any area of my life.

Yet there are a few things that have happened to me that I just don't understand. And even though God has given me light in some dark areas, there are still other things that probably won't be clear to me until I leave this world. And, my wife Nancy and I have suffered significant losses of friends and family, some in tragic circumstances. So, I put my trust, not in this world, but in the One Who said, "Be of good cheer, I have overcome the world" (John 16:33).

Should we expect the unexpected then? Are we to wonder what will happen to us next? Of course not. The Word is sure, and the promises of God are everlastingly true. There *is* a good answer for everything that happens. Yet because of our earthly limitations, we don't always understand, and therefore, there seem to be some "exceptions to the rule." *Don't be shaken and don't be moved.* The "exceptions" are only apparent and not real, for if the law is from God, it is fixed forever. The exceptions *will* pass. The circumstances *will* change. But the Word of God will always endure.

LEARNING FROM JOB

What then can we learn from our brother Job, not just from his good points, but also from his mistakes? Again, the answer is not hard to find, for when Job humbled himself, acknowledged the lordship of God, and repented of his sin, he was healed and restored. When he obeyed the Lord and prayed for his friends, "then the Lord turned the captivity of Job" (Job 42:10; i.e., He restored his fortunes) and gave him twice as much as he had before. Job had gone astray in the middle chapters of the book when he practically challenged God to a face-to-face confrontation. But in chapters 40 and 42, he returned to his original attitude of quiet trust and submission (see Chapters 1 and 2 of this study).

Do you see the point? It never pays to try and force God's hand or put Him on the spot. Actually, many times when we think we're waiting for Him, He is really waiting for us. Waiting for us to stop complaining and whimpering and to get on with the work to which He has called us. He allowed Satan to test His servant Job (and He'll allow that devil to test us too, see Revelation 2:10; for the reality of the battle, see 1 Peter 5:8-9). He even allowed Job and his friends to get into all kinds of speculative discussion and debate (and, of course, we learn from their errors). But when Job finally gave up kicking, the Lord was there to make him well.

In conclusion, then, what do we say when the fiery trials come? "Consider it pure joy, my brothers, whenever you face trials of many kinds, because you know that the testing of your faith develops perseverance" (James 1:2-3). And what do we do when we see inexplicable suffering in the life of a believer? Job spoke of the times when upright men would be horrified over this. Nevertheless, "the righteous will hold fast to his way, and those with clean hands will increase in strength" (Job 17:8-9), "for we walk by faith, not by sight" (2 Corinthians 5:7). Yes, truly, "many are the afflictions of the righteous; but the Lord delivers them out of them all" (Psalm 34:19). Hallelujah! And may the name of the Lord be praised.

***

On February 9, 2011, Nancy sent me an email with quotes from Job, followed by this enthusiastic note: "The important lesson in Job is not that sometimes inexplicable things happens to the righteous, but rather that God does NOT afflict the righteous. What a wonderfully freeing thing to find out that God does not torture His obedient children!!! That was the major problem, the overwhelming obstacle that Job was dealing with. Imagine being a righteous man – walking holy and purely before the Lord, and then imagine being tortured, tormented, inflicted with excruciatingly painful sores or cancers, and then believing that God was the one doing it. What child of God could bear the thought?

One might ask, isn't it the same if God allows the devil to do the afflicting? No, not if He has now given us a way out!

We cannot fully understand the book of Job without the wonderful change that has come about in the New Testament. Before, under the old covenant, God placed a hedge of protection around the righteous, now, under the new covenant, we have been given power and authority over that same enemy that wants to destroy us (Luke 10:18-20: "I saw Satan fall like lightning from heaven. I have given you authority to trample on snakes and scorpions and to overcome all the power of the enemy; nothing will harm you. However, do not rejoice that the spirits submit to you, but rejoice that your names are written in heaven").

The blood of Jesus has delivered us from the enemy. We now have an escape from the afflictions. Jesus said we would have trouble in this world, but to be of good cheer, because He had overcome the world. He said that the devil comes only to steal, kill, and destroy (God showed us that truth in the book of Job), but that He had come to give us life, and give it to the full. The book of Job cannot stand on its own but must be read in light of the New Testament!!!! Thank God!!!

HE KILLS,
BRINGS DOWN,
& DISPOSSESSES
THE WICKED,

BUT HE LIFTS UP
& BLESSES
HIS PEOPLE.

CHAPTER 5

THE JUBILEE HAS COME

So far, we have seen that a right reading of the Old Testament in no way contradicts the message of God's goodness and of faith and healing. Even the Book of Job presents us with no real problems. Satan ripped off God's servant, and after a short (and severe!) time of testing, the Lord gave everything back (with a hint of being reunited with his first ten children in the world to come). In Job's two-hundred-plus years of life (this figure is a rough guess), there was only one momentary, horrific spot of darkness (albeit, with the lasting loss of his first children). The rest of his life was "righteousness, peace, and joy in the Holy Spirit" (Romans 14:17).

But isn't there a difference between the Old and the New Testament? And doesn't this God of ancient Israel seem somewhat different than the God of the Church? Yes, of course. But not because He changed, for He declared in Malachi 3:6: "I am the Lord, I do not change," and James taught us that the heavenly Father "does not change like shifting shadows" (James 1:17). What has changed is the dealings of God with man and the devil. When Jesus came in the fullness of time, God inaugurated His program of restoration. He was about to restore to the world everything that sin had robbed. The jubilee had come.

Everywhere that Jesus went, he undid what Satan had done. When He saw the lost, He saved them. The sick were healed, and the oppressed set free by His hand. The hungry were fed, the bound were loosed, and the maimed made whole through the ministry of Jesus. That is why He came into the world, and His death and resurrection purchased for us a total salvation, redemption of man both now and forevermore.

We are therefore standing on a very different side of the picture than Abraham, Moses, David, and Job. Hebrews 11:39-40 says that "these were all commended for their faith, yet none of them received what was promised. God had planned something better for us so that only together with us would they be made perfect."

Even from the viewpoint of revelation, we are standing on vastly different ground. The truths of resurrection and life-after-death were progressively revealed in the Old Testament, but life and immortality have been totally brought to light through the gospel (2 Timothy 1:10). Religious festivals, new moons, and Sabbaths were only "a shadow of the things that were to come; the reality, however, is found in Christ" (Colossians 2:17).

The character and activity of Satan were revealed gradually in the Old Testament Scriptures. According to 2 Samuel 24:1 (the books of Samuel are very old, dating from about the tenth century BC) the "anger of the Lord" stirred up David to number Israel. But according to 1 Chronicles 21:1, written probably in the fifth century BC, it was Satan who incited David to number the people. In other words, over a five-hundred-year period, there was a progressive revelation of the workings of God and the workings of the devil. Also, aside from the Book of Job and 1 Chronicles 21, Satan is only mentioned by name in the Book of Zechariah, written somewhere in the fifth century BC. And, although the events described in Job are very ancient (i.e., somewhere around 2000 BC, way before the Law was given to Israel), the book itself was not written until much later. (This is based on an analysis of the language of the book and the fact that in the debate between Job and his friends, they are often found to be quoting actual Scriptures written many hundreds of years after their time. In other words, their ancient debate was recast in terms of the language and thought of the age in which the book of Job was written.)

You will remember from the previous chapter that neither Job nor his friends said a word about the devil, nor did they seem to be aware of his existence. Even God Himself said nothing about the enemy's malicious work. Yet the reader of the book was given a glimpse behind the scenes much as the prophet Zechariah was given in chapter 3 of his prophecy. These momentary glimpses into the spiritual realm began to prepare the way for that which was clearly taught in the New Testament: although the Lord God was King of the universe, there was a malignant "kingdom" of evil devoted to the (totally unsuccessful) overthrow of the Kingdom of God. Satan, the god of this world system, is the exact opposite of our loving and gracious Savior. The devil "steals, kills, and destroys"; Jesus gives life, and that "more abundantly" (John 10:10).

Thus, according to the combined revelation of the Old and New Testaments, Satan and his cohorts were obviously God's "agents" of disaster in the inflicting of the Old

Testament punishments and curses. (Of course, I say this in the context of what we learned in chapters 2 and 3. First, in Chapter 3, we learned that God, in revealing Himself to ancient Israel as the one and only God, took full responsibility for these events; and second, in Chapter 2, we learned that His justice demanded, and still demands, that unforgiven sin be punished. On the judgments of God in the New Testament, see, e.g., Acts 5:1-11: Ananias and Saphira; Acts 12:23: Herod is smitten down by the angel of the Lord; Acts 13:10-11: Elymas the sorcerer is struck with blindness; see also Revelation 11:18 and chapters 15-19.) But with the entrance of the Son of God on the earthly scene, the curtains have been totally lifted, and we now see clearly the spiritual warfare in which we are engaged. The good news to the believer is that Jesus has stripped the devil of his power and rendered him ineffective in his attacks on the fully equipped believer.

This "good news" will be the subject of our discussion for the rest of this chapter. But first we must clarify one more point about the activity of "intermediate agents."

Who's Responsible?

All of us, I am sure, have heard of criminal cases in which a "hit man" was hired to kill some unfortunate undesirable. Invariably, when the murderer was apprehended, he was offered a lighter sentence if he would reveal the identity of the individual who hired him. Generally speaking, if this individual is arrested and found guilty, he receives a more severe sentence than the hired killer. Thus, it would appear that the "intermediate agent" who committed the crime is less guilty than the "responsible agent" who planned and masterminded the crime.

This leads us to an obvious question: If God claimed responsibility for the act, why emphasize the activity of an intermediate agent? According to our understanding of justice, the responsible agent bears the brunt of the blame. Therefore, it would seem irrelevant to determine if God Himself killed someone or if in fact it was Satan who was the "hit man."

All this seems reasonable and logical, but it misses something very important. Those who emphasize that "there is no sickness in heaven and therefore God would not put it on His people," do so because they are concerned that the Church have a right understanding of the essential character and nature of God. If we emphasize that God kills, maims, destroys, and afflicts, then we as His children might walk around petrified, not knowing when sudden disaster might hit us. If we emphasize the goodness and mercy of our Father, then we will walk in confidence toward Him.

As for our understanding of God and His agents, here are

two important guidelines. First, we must remember that God only appointed agents of destruction and judgment when justice called for persistent and unrepentant sin to be punished. However, the Lord always disassociated Himself from the wanton cruelty of the destructive agents He appointed. For example, in Isaiah 10:5 God calls Assyria "the rod of My anger," and He says in verse 6, "Against an ungodly nation I send him, and against the people of My wrath I appoint him, to seize the spoil and plunder the booty." But, according to verse 7, "he [i.e., Assyria] doesn't intend to do so, and his mind doesn't think in this way, but rather he plans to destroy and cut off not a few nations." In other words, God sent him to punish Israel for its sins, but instead Assyria arrogantly decided to try and wipe out the world. Thus, we must distinguish between the just actions of God and the cruel actions of the destroying agent, as God said: "I was only angry a little, but they overdid the punishment" (Zechariah 1:15, New Jewish Publication Society Version).

Second, and more importantly, we must not confuse the activity of intermediate agents with the actual character of the Father. The fact that Herod, Pilate, and the nations only fulfilled their predestined plan to reject and crucify Jesus (Acts 4:27-28) does not mean that God, Who ordained the crucifixion, was a murderer. Proverbs 16:4 reads, "The Lord works out everything for His purpose, even the wicked for a day of disaster." Those reading this verse in the KJV ("The Lord hath made all things for Himself; yea, even the wicked for the day of evil") might be misled into thinking that God predestines some people to hell, regardless of their wills or desires. Actually, the Word is teaching us that the Lord will use everyone and everything for His ultimate purpose and plan (Ephesians 1:11).

When it was time for Jesus to die, the Father used ungodly and faithless men to fulfill His plan. When someone's sin merited sudden destruction (see Proverbs 29:1), God used a "destroyer" to carry out the plan. But God is not the destroyer or the murderer or the thief. He is the author of life and peace to His obedient people and the righteous Judge of all. That's why the Word never uses the verb "murder" with reference to God. Murder is the taking of an innocent life without cause; the Lord doesn't do that.

Let me give you one illustration, however, to clarify my point. Imagine that you and your family were at a special communion service being attended by ten thousand believers. Suddenly, at the height of the meeting, five hundred drug-crazed rowdies with sub-machine guns and machetes broke into the crowd threatening to kill everyone present. Quickly they separated the men from the women and children, holding them all at bay with their guns. Then they prepared to kill the men and children and rape and maim the women. Then, just as it seemed that death was near, a believer screamed out, "Save Your people, Lord!" – and instantly, lightning flashed through that building striking the ungodly sinners dead, while not one hair of a single believer was singed.

Naturally you and everyone with you would fall down and worship God, praising and magnifying your Savior and Deliverer. "Thank You, Lord!" you would shout with tears in your eyes. You would not say, "The devil did it," for you would know at once that your help had come from God. Although the destruction wrought by the lightning was awesome and overwhelming it brought life and safety to you. The Lord took life; He did not murder. This parallels the effects of the message of the cross (1 Corinthians 1:18). It is foolishness to those who are perishing (and, therefore, "the smell of death" [2 Corinthians 2:16], but to us who are being saved it is the power of God" [and, thus, "the fragrance of life" (2 Corinthians 2:16)]).

Old Testament scholars like to talk about the "hymnic participles" in the book of Psalms. Now while this term sounds complicated, it is really very simple. "Hymnic" refers to that which is sung in hymns, or songs of praises. "Participles" refer to present tense verbs, verbs of continuous action or doing. In Hebrew, participles were originally nouns, so that the same word for "he writes" also means "writer," and the same word for "he rides" means "rider." The "hymnic participle," therefore, reveals to us the character of God, who He is and what He does. Thus, in Psalm 103 He is spoken of as "He Who forgives sin" (i.e., the Forgiver), "He Who heals diseases" (i.e., the Healer), and "He Who redeems our lives from destruction" (i.e., the Redeemer: 103:3-4; see also 103:5-6). Psalm 147 praises the God Who "builds Jerusalem," "heals the brokenhearted and binds up their pains," and "counts the number of the stars" (147:2-4), again, all "hymnic participles." However, nowhere in the Word is He called, "the One Who bears a grudge," or "the One Who makes us sick," or "the One Who destroys the works of our hands." (In 1 Samuel 2:6-7 we read, "The Lord kills and makes alive; He brings down to Sheol and raises up. The Lord makes poor and makes rich. He casts down, yet He exalts." However, these hymnic participles are to be interpreted in the context of God's just dealings: He kills, brings down, and dispossesses the wicked, but He lifts up and blesses His people.)

Therefore, we must carefully distinguish between the nature of our God, from Whom "every good and perfect gift" comes (James 1:17), and the nature of the agents whom He may utilize. Even when He must exercise Himself in judgment, it is still in holy love that His justice is carried out. This was certainly understood by the Jews of old upon Whom His judgment fell in 586 BC. They did not lay among the ruins of Jerusalem and praise their "heavenly destroyer." Rather, having confessed that they had received the just penalty for their sins, they called on the God Whose mercies were "new every morning" (Lamentations 3:23), even as the prophet cried out, "The Lord is my portion, so says my soul; therefore, I will wait for Him" (Lamentations 3:24).

THE DAY OF RESTORATION

So then, when the fullness of time had come and the people of God had been fully prepared, the Lord inaugurated His restoration program through the preaching of the Kingdom. Jesus said, "The Law and the Prophets were proclaimed until John. Since that time, the good news of the *kingdom of God* is being preached, and everyone is forcing his way into it" (Luke 16:16). The Law and the Prophets, representing the entire Old Testament dispensation, were giving way to the announcement of the coming Kingdom. "For the Law was given through Moses; grace and truth came through Jesus Christ" (John 1:17).

With this in mind, I want to unfold to you a precious truth from the Word. It is impossible to separate the preaching of the gospel from the manifestation of miracles, signs, and wonders, for in its very essence, the gospel is the undoing of all that sin and Satan have done. When Jesus declared to the expectant Jews in Nazareth that Isaiah 61:1 was being fulfilled in their hearing (Luke 4:21), He was referring to the prophetic announcement of the *year of jubilee*, spoken of originally in Leviticus 25. In fact, the phrase "to proclaim freedom (or release)" found in Isaiah 61:1 (and quoted in Luke 4:18) is a virtual quotation of Leviticus 25:10: "proclaim liberty (or release) in all the land." According to Leviticus 25:10, this year of release, or jubilee, to be celebrated once every fifty years, was a time in which *everyone and everything was to return to its original, rightful owner*. Slaves were to be freed, indentured land was to be returned, and debts were to be canceled.

All this was summed up in one Hebrew word, *deror* (pron. d'ROHR), "release," which was translated into Greek by the word *aphesis* (pron. AH-phe-sis), also meaning "release" from a debt or a bound condition. Moreover, in its nuance of "release from the debt of sin," *aphesis* became the standard New Testament word for "forgiveness."

Anyone reading the jubilee chapters of Leviticus would wonder if such a law could ever have been enforced in ancient Israel. Actually, we have no record of a single jubilee ever having been observed in the Old Testament. Nevertheless, the prophets looked for such a miraculous day, although it was to be a day, *not* of merely external cancellation of debts, but rather a day of the cancellation of the debt of sin (see, e.g., Jeremiah 31:34). Therefore, when the Lord spoke prophetically in Isaiah 61:1, He was announcing the eschatological (i.e., end-time) liberation from the plague of sin: "The Spirit of the Lord God is upon me, because the Lord has anointed me to preach good news to the poor. He has sent me to bind up the broken hearted, to proclaim liberty to the captives, and liberation to the prisoners; to proclaim the year of the Lord's favor."

Jesus read these words in front of a tense hometown synagogue crowd in Luke 4, and then He announced, "Today this scripture is fulfilled in your hearing." He was thus inaugurating the coming of God's Kingdom among men. And so, Jesus went everywhere, "proclaiming the good news of God. The time has come," He said. "The kingdom of God is near. Repent and believe the good news!" (Mark 1:14-15).

Look carefully at what transpired immediately *after* Jesus announced Himself in Nazareth (Luke 4:31-43). First, when confronted with a demon-possessed man in Capernaum, He *rebuked* the spirit and cast it out of the man. He was thus correcting and making right what Satan had made wrong. In a word, He was bringing about *restoration*. Second, Jesus encountered Peter's mother-in-law suffering from a high fever. As recorded in Luke's gospel, and only Luke's gospel, He *rebuked* the fever, "and it left her." Once again, *restoration* was accomplished. No prayers offered, no petitions submitted, only words spoken — *restoration words.* By rebuking that which was wrong, He made room for that which was right.

That evening, the crowds came to Jesus, "and he drove out the spirits with a word and healed all the sick" (Matt. 8:16). When the people tried to keep him from leaving, Jesus said, "I must preach the *good news of the kingdom of God* to the other towns also, because that is why I was sent" (Luke 4:43, my italics). He healed the sick, cast out demons, and set captives free, but according to the Word, all this was only the outward manifestation of the preaching of the good news of the Kingdom. Where God's Kingdom goes, Satan's kingdom falls, sin's strongholds are broken, the devil's prison house is opened, and the captives march out free in God.

Look at this amazing series of verses linking the preaching of the Kingdom with the miracles of God: "Jesus went throughout Galilee, teaching in their synagogues, preaching the good news of the kingdom, and healing every disease and sickness among the people" (Matthew 4:23; compare Matthew 9:35). "These twelve Jesus sent out with the following instructions . . . . 'As you go, preach this message: "The Kingdom of heaven is near." Heal the sick, raise the dead, cleanse those who have leprosy, drive out demons'" (Matthew 10:5,7,8). Jesus said to the Pharisees: "If I drive out demons by the Spirit of God, then the kingdom of God has come upon you" (Matthew 12:28; cf. Luke 11:27). The driving out of demonic spirits by God's Spirit is thus proof of the presence of a greater kingdom, the Kingdom of God.

In answer to the disciples of John the Baptist, Jesus responded, "Go back and report to John what you hear and see: The blind receive sight, the lame walk, those who have leprosy are cured, the deaf hear, the dead are raised, and the good news is preached to the poor" (Matthew 11:4-5). And what is this good news? The Kingdom of God has come, and according to Isaiah 35, miracles of healing and restoration proclaim the good news that God has come to save His people (see Isaiah 35:1-10).

Jesus told His disciples that the "gates of hell" themselves could not prevail against the church (Matthew 16:18), and in the ancient world, a city's gates represented its strength and glory. As great as the city's gates were, so great was its power and prestige. Yet when the Church of Jesus Christ marches right up to the very gates of hell to the very heart and soul of the enemy's power, those defensive weapons will be powerless in their efforts to stop our onslaught.

Satan's kingdom stands wherever men and women enthrone him as their master. His gates are locked round about them, and they have no way out. But when the light of the gospel shines forth, the devil's defenses are shattered, and a mighty host of the redeemed marches out. This great deliverance began when Jesus spoiled the forces of darkness by His death on the cross and His resurrection from the grave. It continues wherever the Kingdom of God is proclaimed in power: sin's captives are loosed and become free children of the living Lord.

In Jesus's great commission to His disciples, He declared that repentance and forgiveness of sins would be preached in His name to all nations, beginning at Jerusalem (see Luke 24:47). The Greek word for "forgiveness" is again *aphesis* — release from the debt of sin. This then was the message that changed the world, and it will be the message that ushers in the Lord's return. The debt of sin has been canceled by the death of God's Son on the cross, *therefore by faith we can be free from all that sin brought into the world*, beginning here and culminating in the world to come. Death itself has lost its sting, for after a short "rest" even our bodies will be resurrected. Jesus the Victor has conquered all!

From everlasting to everlasting, God has had a plan. He created a universe full of glory and beauty, with an innumerable company of angels to serve Him, and a race of unique beings to have fellowship with Him. Throughout history the Lord was working towards the fulfillment of His great plan, from creation to the fall, from the calling of Abraham and his seed to the giving of the Law, right on through the entire Old Testament and up until the time of Jesus and the founding of the Church. Finally, at the end of this age, the eternal purpose of God will reach its culmination in time – the kingdoms of this world will become the Kingdom of our God, and He will reign forever (Revelation 11:15).

From the time of the infancy of this universe to the time of its renewal, there will have been only one God and only one plan. In His marvelous wisdom and power, He prepared a people for Himself and revealed His will to them. Throughout their recorded history He endeavored to reveal Himself to them and to open their eyes to the crucial fact that there is only one God, Yahweh, the Lord. In the fullness of time, He entered this world in human flesh, God incarnate, the mystery of the ages. The Lord Jesus walked among us, and by His sinless life and substitutionary death He paid for the sins of man. We who were once alienated from the Lord by our wicked works now have perfect fellowship with our heavenly Father. We are no longer "children of wrath" destined for destruction; we have become fellow-heirs with the Beloved Son, destined for immortality.

The Compassionate Father, perfect in justice. The Consuming Fire, perfect in mercy. Now you know the God of the Old TestamentThe Compassionate Father, perfect in justice. The Consuming Fire, perfect in mercy. Now you know the God of the Old Testament.

Please Stay Connected with Me!

We are active on social media and have thousands of hours of free resources available at our website, AskDrBrown.org. Receive our weekly, informative emails, then connect with me on Facebook, Twitter, YouTube, or Instagram. I look forward to being in touch!

P.S. We also have a full-time, online ministry training program. Check out FIRE School of Ministry today!

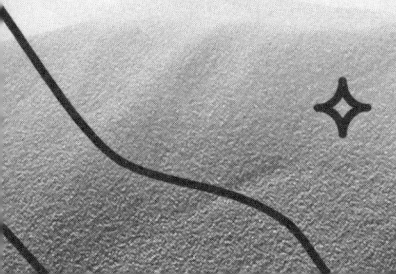

JOB: THE FAITH
TO CHALLENGE GOD
A NEW TRANSLATION AND COMMENTARY

Just as there was no man on earth like Job, there is no book on earth like the book of Job. In this new commentary, biblical scholar Michael Brown brings Job to life for the twenty-first-century reader, exploring the raw spirituality of Job, his extraordinary faith, his friends' theological errors, the mysteries of God's speeches, and the unique answers to the problem of suffering offered in the book of Job.

BOOKS CAN BE PURCHASED FROM ASKDRBROWN.ORG

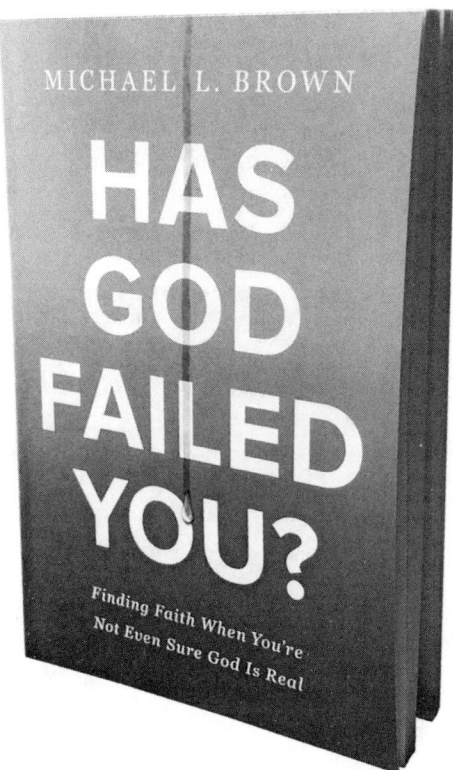

HAS GOD FAILED YOU?

FINDING FAITH WHEN YOU'RE NOT EVEN SURE GOD IS REAL

As some well-known Christians announce a newfound loss of faith, other believers face increasing pressure or doubt. We feel let down, ashamed to question God's goodness, and in need of assurance of our faith and answers to our pain. This book presents a frank and insightful discussion about whether or not it's okay to doubt God and what to do about it.

BOOKS CAN BE PURCHASED FROM ASKDRBROWN.ORG